NONE OF US ARE SUPERMAN

SANE SEVEN

Book Design: Jurga Skeiryte
Proofing: Dawn Collinson & Janet Tansley (Copy Media)
Interviews: Debbie Johnson

ISBN 978-0-9956996-0-1

Printed and bound in Hong Kong
by Great Wall Printing Co. Ltd.

CONTENTS

ACKNOWLEDGEMENTS

This book would be one page long without the dedication of **Debbie Johnson**, a brilliant journalist and writer who worked on this book with us for the past two years without eating, sleeping or breathing. None of us are Superman but she was close to flying using her laser sharp observations and superhuman ability to record extensive details to fill the pages of the book with these brilliant features. We are eternally grateful for your hard work and we'll always remember and laugh at those missed calls, frustrating delays, comments that nobody will even know about and things we never said out loud when things didn't go as planned. Thank you for sharing the time you could have spent with your family or working on another one of your brilliant novels.

The book would be much less exciting without **Viktorija Grigorjevaite's** creative genius (and unpronounceable surname). Never ask her for an advice about what a good business portrait needs because you'll end up with a duck in your hands or a horse in your living room, or worse, in the police custody for using smoke grenades in public space. Her exceptional portraits turned the book into a fine art album. There were plenty of 'oh shit' and 'damn it' moments to make an exciting documentary from behind the scenes. From lights falling down in the rain to corrupted files, angry location owners, and sunrises on the way of a long drives home.

The book would be even shorter than one page without each and every individual who participated in the book. We didn't dare to ask how much a minute of your time cost but we valued every moment we spent with you. Thank you for all the cups of tea, warm welcome, interesting stories, honesty, introductions, advice and of course Beethoven's Sonata No 14 (it was flawless). We did our best not to misrepresent your views in the book but we will be checking our post box for a note from your lawyers.

We would also like to thank **Jurga Skeiryte** for suffering our caprices when designing the book. Thank you for numerous revised versions and constant changes. We apologise to your son Lukas for taking so much of his mother's time away from him.

Grace Woods, thank you for traveling with us to the photo shoots. Your make up was so good that some men probably still wear it a year later.

We are grateful to Kevin McManus for support the project throughout the two years in a making. Thank you for always finding the time to offer help and advice despite your numerous other commitments as a guru of creative, digital and music realms.

We are grateful to the owners of the following locations for letting us use their space to create some of the beautiful portraits: Hope Street Hotel, Doncaster Airport, Lodge Riding Centre, Belle Vue Stadium in Manchester.

Finally, we would like to thank the following individuals for their extra special kind of support: **Chris Bliss, Andrew Collinge, Dominic Burke, George Davies, George Downing, Ian Ayre, Ian Meadows, Kevin Morley, The Earl of Derby, Max Steinberg, Sir Michael Bibby, Nick Earlam, Peter Johnson, Phil Millward, Asif Hamid, Steve Morgan, Judy Halewood.**

PRELUDE TO SUCCESS

by Marius J., PhD

In our society, we treat successful business leaders as superhuman: distant, divine and composed of such celestial energy that the rest of us can only dream of.

They stand on their gold-plated pedestals, automatically respond to every question with the perfect answer, and they always know what will happen before it happens. They have what it takes – a mythical set of personal qualities, experience and instinct which simply makes them better than anyone else.

For most of us, this ideal can feel unattainable. We struggle through our working lives, frustrated and confused, wondering why that seemingly brilliant business idea is not delivering the expected results, why everything seems to take much longer, and why even the simplest things act like square wheels on an otherwise perfect car - fruitless advertising, small web traffic, problematic employees and passive investors. Sometimes we all wonder if we really have what it takes, if there is still potential in us, if it isn't too late and if it is worth, even, to try.

Potential vs. performance

You don't know what you are capable of, until you stretch yourself to the limit *(Robert Hough)*

It can be easy to conclude that you are on the wrong train and in the wrong seat, especially after a failed business attempt or another day stuck in a dead-end job. That feeling comes like an angry conductor, convincingly insisting that your ticket is not valid and that it's time for you to get off. Not knowing what the right next step should be, not trusting your instincts, feeling unsure, not having a winning plan, feeling like you're winging it, flying by the seat of your pants - surely these are not the qualities that will one day help you pass the £1bn revenue mark, turn you into a CEO of an international company, or earn you the Order of the British Empire?

And if that doesn't deter you from scrambling for success, compare yourself with those who have been there, done that – the Bransons, Zuckerbergs and Oprahs of the business world. Along with everything they say and do, there is a 10-volume encyclopedia delineating 1001 ways in which their decisions and actions outdo everything you've ever attempted.

But what does it really say about you and your chances of succeeding in business, life, or career?

We often see successful people at the peak of their careers, in their fully-formed glory. It can be easy to forget that all peaks start in valleys and successful people are no exception. At the start of their journeys they themselves had little in common with who they are today. Comparing ourselves with them at the peak of their abilities is like looking for commonalities between a buried seed and a blooming tree. At best, you can compare your opinion about your abilities with their 15 years of choices and decisions which made them who they are.

Time has a way of turning potential into performance but we often see time as our enemy, not as an ally. As babies, we never thought we could walk, talk, or recite an eight times table but we had the potential to. As 10-year-olds, we couldn't drive a car, hold down a job, or live independently from our parents, but we had the potential to. Now, regardless of our age, the nature or status of our businesses, we are at the beginning of the next stretch of 10-15 years that could reveal something new, something remarkable and unexpected about us. The difference is that what will happen next depends on what we believe could happen next, and whether we take steps towards it.

Our opinion about our ability to change may well be the only thing that will determine whether we rise, fall or stop. It's whether we accept the possibility that 10-15 years of our own choices and decisions could turn focused effort into a multi-million pound industry, even if we don't feel that we have what it takes to build or manage it today.

We cannot predict what will happen in our future, but we can at least count on change; count on the fact that we may not know how to do something now but reach for it knowing that, by the time we get there, we will have the skill to see things through.

Standardisation of success

None of us really knows what qualities we have, especially in terms of these kinds of business-related skills. There isn't an objective yardstick to judge it by (Sir Terry Leahy)

Imagine an ultimate business course that promises to help you build a successful business. It will tell you all you need to know, every strategy you need to use and every step you need to take. Four prospective business owners attend the course. Their names are Windows, Linux, Mac OS and Google Chrome. They all get the secret manual of success called secrets_of_success.exe.

We all know how the story ends. Linux ends up working in McDonald's, Mac OS convinces herself that she never really had any big dreams, and Google Chrome thinks the course was a bit weak. Ten years later they all read about Windows in Forbes. Everyone concludes that Windows 'had what it takes' to see things through because of some special qualities she had. Others have tried but they have failed, they were not good enough to grasp the concepts, to follow the standard model of success. Nobody thought that the most popular path wasn't the optimal path for who they were.

This fictional story is not so far-fetched. In reality, our abilities are always judged with reference to the most popular opinion, the most confident 'expert', the loudest-shouting member in a group, or the latest trending yardstick – the one size fits all approach. Sometimes that comparison can be very persuasive in convincing us that somebody else knows better who we are and how we function.

The role of individual differences is often underplayed or overlooked in our society. From the earliest days we have been fed the opinion that success lies at the end of a standard path - a thin invisible line that has no name or coordinates. We are taught to walk that line in school by taking standard exams, performing standard tests, and being rewarded for behaving in standard ways. Those results determine whether universities will see you as having potential, employers will look at university results to judge how good you are. If you don't have the right numbers, you don't have what it takes. We've always been taught to be the most standard and most average members of society. Any variation is seen as deviation from the norm, the less optimal option.

Such tendency to look for one general way, an abstract formula, or a theory of everything is also evident in the way we define successful people. For example, the Internet teeming with seductive headlines claiming to have found what makes someone a success: '9 qualities that make a great business leader', '10 habits of business leaders', '8 leadership traits'. These features imply that because 10 habits/ traits or characteristics are shared by successful people, they are the reason why they are successful.

However, if this is the case, if these traits make them successful above their personal circumstances or situations, then swapping two people who share these qualities should ensure their success in any situation. Such people should be interchangeable.

For example, if Warren Buffet and Mark Zuckerberg swapped their places, would they be equally successful because they share some general principles of success or would they be less than ideal because it's more about something specific to each individual and each situation? If it's the latter, does the former even matter if those principles are not general enough to ensure success?

A success formula clearly needs more detailed description. But this creates an interesting paradox. The longer and more detailed the formula, the less likely it is to apply to every successful individual. In turn, the shorter the 'formula', the less likely that it will ensure success. In other words, if someone's success is too complex to describe in a way that would apply to another person, then their secret of success is a unique summary of their whole life.

As similar as some may like to think we are to each other, we all come with different experiences and biological compositions that turn us into completely different 'information processing machines'. Not just PCs or Macs but six billion individuals who make sense of the world differently, function differently, and need different things to motivate us.

We can all learn the same theories but we can't all be the same person. While it makes our journeys less predictable and much more uncertain, you can at least be sure that you have the one asset that nobody else has access to − you. It's just a matter of finding out what makes you the most awkward piece of a puzzle in the standard model of success.

Success will always be a mysterious path. But in the words of Kung Fu Panda, sometimes the best path is not the one that works for others but the one that taps into your own strengths. Sometimes it means that the path is to be the fattest ninja, not the wisest turtle.

ABOUT THE BOOK

From the stories that began in the toughest suburbs and ended in the multi-billion pound companies, to the stories that highlighted the upside of literally telling your own boss to 'f*@! off'... this unpretentiously honest, beautifully illustrated, and engagingly written book delves into the secrets of success by picking the brains of 33 very different charismatic business leaders.

They have built more than 80,000 houses, boasted revenues of £1bn, appeared in South Park, become household names, headed Liverpool FC, Rolls Royce and Bentley, and turned Tesco into the international giant we know it as. Now they invite you to reflect on your own potential and abilities, engaging in the discussion about what 'having what it takes' really means.

Presented without censorship and extensive editing, these exclusive features will reveal how time and experience changes business personality and ambitions. You will learn how digging sewers can lead to building a FTSE 250 company, and how a couple of bad starts are no obstacles to turning yourself into a household name like George at Asda.

You will get the sense of a timescale of building a successful career, learning what decisions can lead someone to becoming CEO of one of the largest insurance brokers in the world or a PE teacher rising as the face of a multi-billion dollar gaming giant, Electronic Arts.

Other features will show that no title or family name comes with inborn business knowledge, whether it is taking over one of the biggest family businesses in Britain or inheriting a role of historical importance.

You will discover how not having a great plan can help you amass a £1bn property portfolio, and how flying by the seat of your pants can earn you the title of the most influential person in the electronic dance music industry.

You will also learn that no individual is exempt from biological and psychological laws of nature and how self-criticism, fears and emotions in general are inseparable parts of the success journey.

Finally, you will realise that no two leaders are the same, and that different leaders demonstrate different pitfalls and shortcuts as being important to building a successful and sustainable business.

We hope that the book will help you find inspiration, brilliant quotes and the elements that will help you tell your own success story.

PETER MOORE

Peter Moore was raised as the son of a publican in some of Liverpool's toughest neighbourhoods – and now he is the public face of a multi-billion dollar company. His career reads like the American dream: from starting as a shoe salesman in 1982, he ends up as president of Patrick USA by 1988. From only knowing video games via his son, he goes on to launch the Sega Dreamcast and the Xbox 360, and be the COO of gaming and entertainment giant Electronic Arts. From being a humble PE teacher in North Wales, he evolves into one of the most well-known business figures in the world – earning him his very own appearance in South Park.

He's the mastermind behind some of the world's best-known brands, acted as a driving force in huge global companies, and worked closely with Bill Gates. He's also been at the centre of some now legendary, but entirely true, stories including the time in Tokyo he told his boss at Sega to 'go fuck himself', and the infamous Xbox Red Ring of Death affair.

It might read like a film script but nobody, no matter how lucky, starts off living in a pub in Speke and ends up driving an Aston Martin Vanquish around California without a lot of hard work, talent, and some unique characteristics. Here Peter Moore shares his journey, and his thoughts on what made it so eventful.

I always think there are only five or six big decisions you face in life which really matter. They often involve risk and can define your entire future.

For me, the first major change came when I was working as a PE teacher in Llangollen. It was freezing cold, and I'd been teaching for four years. I got a call from a former professor offering me the chance to move to California and coach soccer. I'd been working in the States during my summers and felt very drawn to the American way of life and its inherently positive attitude, especially compared to Britain in the 70s.

So my then girlfriend, later wife, Bernice and I packed up and moved to the US – I left a solid, respectable job as a teacher and took that initial risk. Don't get me wrong, it wasn't all easy. Those first 18 months were probably the hardest of my life. We were living in a trailer with no running water, and I was working for a few dollars an hour and studying for my Masters at night so I could stay on a student visa. And when Bernice got pregnant, the risk became even higher – we couldn't afford for her to have a baby in the States, so at seven months pregnant, I waved her off on the plane back to the UK (and the NHS) in her big coat to hide her baby bump, and stayed behind in Long Beach.

By that time I had a job selling footwear for Patrick. It was commission only so if I didn't sell, I didn't earn. I drove literally hundreds of miles around my patch, using the 'gifts' I had to make it work – optimism, self-confidence and a belief that it was all going to work out. Some of that I definitely developed during my childhood – we lived in pubs on Scotty Road and Speke, later moving to Wales, where I was a foreigner and forever known as 'Scouse'.

I worked in the pubs from being a kid, and it's there I learned some of the skills I still rely on today. I had to talk to the customers, serve their needs, joke with them, play darts with them. Later, when I was teaching, I had to use those same skills to persuade a load of kids, day in day out, that they really did want to learn, and ultimately the skills you use in business are the same ones. The definition of a business is putting customers in touch with the products they want or need, in a way that is profitable to your company, your employees, your clients and your stakeholders. That remains true – whether you're selling beer or video games – and if you master those skills early on, and hone them over time, they won't fail you or let you down.

So, as I'm driving around California selling shoes, using my gift of the gab and unveiling the Kevin Keegan Gold soccer shoe like it was priceless art, I also chose to immerse myself in my surroundings. This is another of the keys to good business in my opinion: pay attention. Look at what is going on around you. I absorb a lot of detail very quickly, which you need to do in business – stay on your toes, stay alert, let it all seep in through osmosis. For me, this was also cultural in those early days. I didn't want to be one of those ex-pats who forever thinks baseball is like rounders; I wanted to understand it, to grasp it, to be part of it. I bought a house near Compton, laid down roots.

Moving from a commission sales rep to the president of the company didn't happen by accident – it happened because of results. It happened because I made it happen, and because I was working in an American environment that responded to working your ass off, no matter what your class or background or accent.

I moved from there to Reebok and brokered the deal with Liverpool FC, which is one of my proudest achievements – being able to combine my past and my present. While I was there, eventually as senior vice president of global marketing, I was approached by a recruiter about a role with Sega. "Have you heard of Sega?" he asked. "Yeah," I replied, "I think my son plays their games."

The worst decision you can make is no decision at all – if you freeze, you lose.

I was 44 years old, and that was about the sum total of my knowledge of that industry, so this was another one of those big decisions. The

Everyone fails
sometimes, but
what counts is
the way you
handle it.

time when I had to decide whether to take a risk or not – whether my optimism and self-belief were enough to take me into a whole new world; whether it was time to hit the reset button and move into an industry that I could see was going to explode. I said yes, and I've worked in gaming ever since.

By this stage, I suppose I had a good idea of what I think makes a successful business person, or a successful person, full stop. Decisiveness is essential – our world, especially mine, works at internet speed. You have to see what needs doing, and get it done; don't leave it a few days and hope for the best. Get it done. The worst decision you can make is no decision at all – if you freeze, you lose.

Empathy is also essential. I don't have any time for what I call 'command and control' types who sit in their corner offices, sending out emails and orders. If you don't understand your customers, you won't succeed. If you don't understand your workforce, you'll lose great employees. You need to be involved, you need to know how hard they're working, their thoughts, and their aspirations. If you miss out on all of that, they can, and will, abandon you.

Finally, you need to focus on the results. These aren't always financial, but they are never subjective – getting results should drive everything you do in business. That focus, for me, started when I was putting in all those miles in my Toyota Camry, selling shoes for Patrick and being pleased with a thousand dollars of sales. Now, at EA, we can have $150M launch days, but the focus is still the same. Get the results. Hustle, work hard, pay attention. Get it done.

That same focus comes into play when things aren't going well, and I haven't worked for this long without things going wrong. I've had plenty of 'oh shit' moments – everyone fails sometimes, but what counts is the way you handle it.

The first thing is to anticipate it – analyse risk, be prepared, whether it's your own start-up or a multi-billion dollar company. See the holes before you fall into them, and don't panic. If you see a $40m gap in revenue on the horizon, don't stick your head in the sand, confront it and look at how you'll fix it. I heard a phrase on American radio not long after I moved there – EGBOK. It means Everything's Going To Be Okay. When you see a failure on the horizon, don't shy away, believe in yourself. Believe that EGBOK.

That might sound flippant, but I've been there, a few times. When I got into a dispute with my Japanese bosses at Sega – and eventually told them to go fuck themselves (literally) – I was convinced that I'd be okay. And I was right – I ended up at Microsoft.

There, I faced one of the toughest situations of my career: a product fault with the Xbox 360 that became known as the Red Ring of Death. We started so well with the launch, we were on fire with it, but then the calls started coming in about a problem with the console. A few calls turned into hundreds, and eventually we realised there was a major issue. The problem wasn't my fault, but I was accountable. I had to fix it.

We sat down and looked at what was happening, and what we needed to do – if we didn't fix it, Xbox would have been dead, simple as that. We evaluated the cost of getting all those units back, repairing them, sending out new ones, keeping our customers happy, keeping the brand alive. It came to $1.15billion. Now, that was an 'oh shit' moment, having to go in and see my boss and tell him that. Of course I was worried – I thought I might get fired! Plus there was the fear that Microsoft – who basically print money with their other products, and didn't really need gaming – would just pull the plug on the whole thing.

They didn't – they faced the problem, admitted it, and fixed it. That is good business.

There have been times when my optimism has been challenged, of course there have. I'm not a machine. I had to oversee the transition of Sega from the hardware business after Dreamcast ended, and that was a very humbling experience. I had to make 50 people redundant, many of whom I had personally brought with me from Reebok. That was extremely tough, and the flip side of the empathy that you need to succeed is being aware of the human impact of your decisions. Wherever I could, I made those calls myself, but it was very tough indeed.

And my self-confidence isn't unassailable. When I started at Microsoft, I felt overwhelmed by it all to begin with. I mean, I've never taken a business class in my life – I'm trained as a PE teacher! Everything I'd learned, I'd learned through my own personal and professional experience, and I suddenly found myself working in this massive organisation. I didn't understand 'code', I wasn't one of them. I was sitting in a room with Bill Gates, the smartest individual I've met in my life.

But I paid attention and I showed up. In some ways, early on, there was an element of bullshit involved. Winging it. Fake it until you make it … But saying you're 'bullshitting' does it a disservice – to do that, you need to have paid attention, learned, be reliable, honour your commitments. Even bullshitting can have a solid foundation.

Over the years, at all these companies, I've worked with so many people and I've learned what I admire, and what I don't. I am very judgmental, I tend to make snap decisions which aren't always right, but usually are. The things that impress me in a person are simple: have your act together, be able to prioritise what you need to do in life, recognise the big moments and grasp them. If you're starting out in business, and you have a big meeting coming up, put everything else on hold – you make sure you are 100% prepared, ready for it, ready to make the most of any opportunities. Don't complain about it, just get on with it, because at the end of the day you're doing it to change your own life.

When my dad was running pubs in Speke and Scotland Road, and he didn't think it was the right environment in which to raise his family, he got off his arse and got a new pub in Wales. He made his disadvantages – being an outsider – an advantage, made being a Scouser his 'schtick'. If you look out of the window and you're not happy, do something to change it – don't just go to the pub and whinge to your mates about how shitty your life is. If you feel disappointed by what life has given you, change it, make it to your advantage, use it as motivation.

That said, ambition needs to have foundation. When I'm judging others, one thing I often see is people moving too far, too fast. I'll look at people's resumes and see they've done five jobs in three years. They've been overly ambitious – remember you can learn something from every environment. Get a few wins, establish yourself, don't push yourself into incompetency.

At one stage I suspected I'd done that myself. I was at Microsoft and was offered a position with EA SPORTS. I know sports, I love sports, and I was by then a seasoned video game professional, so it seemed the right move, especially as it was back to California. I've dragged my family all over the States – San Francisco, Seattle, Boston – it's the American way. Chase your career, no matter where you have to move to succeed …

So, I go there as president of EA SPORTS. It's a good fit – until before too long, I was offered the job as COO of EA. I was worried, it was outside my comfort zone and I wondered if I was breaking my own rule and going too far, too fast. But I took it and it was another of those big decisions.

I'm 61 now, and have the experience to look back over my life and see things more clearly. The way you view things as you get older changes. When you're a kid, life revolves around planning for next Friday. When you start your career, it might be a year from now. Then if you are results orientated, you start to reverse engineer from the future – where do I want to be with this in three years' time, and how do I get there?

As important as all of this is, you also need to make time to press pause – slow down every now and then and appreciate what life has given you. You don't want to miss out on the good stuff. I think the person I am now is a combination of what I was born with, early experience, and the things I've learned along the way.

I was inspired by good examples – hard working parents who were so busy working, they made me and my brothers and sister very independent. Working in a pub and meeting all kinds of different people. Having a great PE teacher who inspired a love of team sports and the mentalities behind it that can help you in life. Going into teaching myself. I can see the DNA strands, I can see the early building blocks – but then as you progress through life, you learn to understand yourself better, see the way things work and know how to best operate. Again, if you pay attention, you never stop learning. Eventually, you can add to those early building blocks yourself.

It's hard to imagine when you are starting out in business, but success doesn't make you immune to problems. Even if you are at the upper end of your profession, there will always be challenges. EA, for example, is now making the transformation into an entirely digital concern. It's taken a human toll. There was a lot of attrition, remixing of skills. We didn't come out of it unscathed, but we HAVE come out of it and are now flourishing.

I'm still facing the same pressures I did in the early days – the need to keep coming up with results. I still need to have that focus, drive and ambition. I still need to have empathy and self-confidence. I still need to believe that everything will be okay. EGBOK …

GEORGE DAVIES

Risk / People / Learn / Opportunity / Understanding

From a would-be professional footballer to a potential dentist, George Davies had a few false starts before finding his passion for fashion – and going on to launch some of the UK's best-known brands. Dubbed the King of the High Street, this award-winning businessman is estimated to have sold well over £50bn worth of clothing since the launch of Next in the 1980s. A household name via Asda, the man behind Per Una, and now spearheading FG4 around the Middle East, George is as ambitious as ever. Here he shares his views on business, retail, and trusting your own vision.

Looking back on my career, and the things that shaped me, I'd have to say that a love of sport is right up there on the list.

When I was growing up, there was loads of open space, and I was always out and about playing football. I loved football, and golf, and all kinds of sports. You can't be a success in sport, or in business I don't think, without a competitive spirit – you have to want to succeed, to be the best, to win, to lead. With me, that showed itself early on with sport but I don't think I've ever lost it. Like with sport though, it's important to remember to shake hands after the match!

I think that's a natural attribute, and one most entrepreneurs have – a desire to push yourself. In terms of my working life though, it took a while to find a place where it could really take hold. My mum wanted me to make something of myself and I went off to university to study dentistry. It didn't quite take, and I left. I always had a work ethic – I've delivered bread, been a milkman, you name it – and I was never lazy, but I knew that I was never going to be a dentist, no matter how good a career it was. It took getting a job at Littlewoods to find what I was passionate about.

> **If you don't love what you're doing, how can you expect other people to?**

My mum and her family used to make their own clothes, and she was a very strong influence in my life, so maybe it was there beneath the surface all along. It was completely accidental though, that I ended up working in clothing and retail. I needed a job after deciding against dentistry and I applied to both Pilkington and Littlewoods as they were the big employers around Liverpool at the time. I didn't really have any strong leanings towards either to be honest, I was only really applying to keep my mother happy. With hindsight, I suppose everything could have gone very differently if I'd ended up at Pilkington!

At Littlewoods though, I discovered that I absolutely loved the world of retail and fashion. I was lucky enough to get chosen for a Design and Buyers course that came with fantastic training, a real solid grounding in the fashion industry – the kind of training it's hard to come by these days. It was the start of everything for me, and I think it highlights something very important – you need to find your passion.

It's far better in the longer term to be doing a job or working in a business that you love rather than one you don't, regardless of money or how well you can 'get on'. Without that passion, without adoring what you do, you won't be motivated, and you'll never develop a real understanding of the world you're working in – without loving something, you won't fully be able to understand your market, your customers, your environment. And if you don't love what you're doing, how can you expect other people to?

Starting there, at the very bottom, also taught me lots of other skills – how to deal with being at the bottom of the pecking order, how to cope with being the butt of everyone's sense of humour (which makes you very resilient!) and how to soak up every bit of experience life throws at you. You can learn a lot at university or at school, but you learn even more from real life. You learn how to mix with people from all backgrounds, you learn how to take and how to make a joke, you learn about life.

> You learn a lot more in adversity than you do when everything is going your way.

I would always recommend that young people, if they can, take a gap year, work abroad, experience different cultures, or pursue something worthwhile here. It's absolutely invaluable. It's not wasted – it all helps give you a better understanding of how the world works and can also help you better appreciate your potential markets and customers in a way that academic learning can't. Working in a big, competitive organisation like Littlewoods, when I was young, was the making of me.

Littlewoods was my launch pad, really – but there came a point where I had to decide to take a risk. All business involves risk, and if you don't want a life that involves any risk, then business probably isn't the best route for you. It's all a balance between deciding what risks are worth it, when to take them, how much to risk, and how to cope when it doesn't pay off! I always think you learn a lot more in adversity than you do when everything is going your way – it's certainly been true for me. It's when things go wrong that you start to accumulate some wisdom.

In my late 20s, I decided to take what was probably the biggest risk of my life – I started my own mail order schoolwear business. At the time, I was helping to build my own house, I had a decent job and a bit of equity behind me. I spotted a gap in the market for selling cheaper schoolwear and went for it. I learned a lot very quickly – mainly the double-edged sword that is running your own small business. I went from a big set-up like Littlewoods to being on my own and I had to learn a lot, from A-Z, very fast!

> **It's those times when risk goes sour that you have to dig deepest, and you see what you're really made of.**

It was a risk and it seemed to be paying off – until it almost went disastrously wrong. I had borrowed some backing money from a bank that eventually got into trouble and went bust. All the capital from the business, all the takings and profits, went with it – I lost it all.

The business itself was doing well, and the concept was working. I'd not been wrong to take the risk but, as ever with life, sometimes unexpected things happen. So I'd built this business, and I had employees, and I really didn't want to see it all disappear – but the money was simply gone, along with the bank. What was I going to do?

I wanted to fight to save it, that was my instant reaction – and it's those times when risk goes sour that you have to dig deepest, and you see what you're really made of. For me, I work best under pressure, when I'm stressed, my brain seems to work better! It's when everything's flowing along easily that I have problems!

So I was offered an opportunity – to merge with a company called Rosgill Holdings, who sold under the name Pippa Dee. In some ways it wasn't ideal – we all had to move to Burton on Trent and we were living in pubs to start with! – but it was an opportunity to save the business. And, as it turned out, it was an opportunity to do much more. It was a business ripe for development and, again, I was able to make a real difference, and play with some good ideas. Pippa Dee products were sold by 15,000 women across the UK and, within five or six years, I was able to turn the whole business around.

So ultimately, taking a risk did pay off – and so did that risk going wrong! Perhaps that's easier to say with hindsight, but it did work out – and you need to believe that things will, even when they go wrong.

I think one of the other things that helped me in my career was something I was told when I started at Littlewoods: it's all about social development. Now, at the time, I don't think I fully understood it – but it's something that has been invaluable, certainly in fashion and retail, and I think in all business. It's about looking at the world and the culture around you, seeing what's changing, what is about to change, and ways you can fit into that and find a gap in the market.

Selling schoolwear, for example, was partly a response to the change from grammar schools to comprehensives. At Pippa Dee, which sold via home parties run by women, I realised that the fact that it was so popular showed there was a gap in the retail market – so by the time I was approached to develop what eventually became Next, I had a thorough understanding of the social development in retail. I spent ages studying different stores in 25-30 different towns and finding shops that were badly designed, poorly stocked, and concentrating entirely on a disposable youth market – not the slightly more mature women that Next would cater for.

Same with George at Asda – people in London struggled with the 'out of town' concept, with the whole idea of a supermarket on the outskirts of a town, or on a retail park, that would also sell clothes. But I saw it as a great opportunity: social development told me that these out-of-town stores would become bigger and bigger, and providing high-quality fashion for the family was the way forward. People could buy clothes that they loved at a price they could afford at a place that was convenient.

Spotting that social development – and the way it might affect your product, market or business – is absolutely essential. I think some of that is natural but some of it is definitely out there to be learned. All of it, ultimately, is also about trusting your own vision. It's about believing that what you are offering, or what you are planning, is of value and will succeed. Sometimes you have to fight for that – I once had to go home to my wife, when we had three kids and a mortgage, and tell her I might be out of a job! But that was just before the opportunity with Next came along, and I think it's fair to say that trusting my own vision worked.

As time has moved on I don't think my basic principles have changed – I still believe in being competitive; in striving to succeed, in knowing your customer and knowing their culture, whether that is in the UK in the 80s or the Middle East in the 21st century. I still believe you need to be passionate about what you are creating, about the brand you are selling, before you can expect anybody else to be. None of that has really changed – it's just that there are a few more challenges thrown in now, like the pace and scale at which communications have changed.

All of this has worked for me – and along the way, I've also seen the things that haven't worked. I've been in business with lots of different people, been part of many different organisations and companies, and I think the one thing that consistently is a major shortcoming in senior managers is their failure to create a team culture.

In all the time I've been in business, I've not had an office – I still don't. I sit out there, with everybody else. I understand what's going on, I understand my people. I believe very firmly in caring for my team, in offering them the same opportunities I had, to have a career, to have good training. I want them to be inspired – to feel they are working with me, not for me.

People who forget all of that, who stop being hands-on for whatever reason – maybe they never were, or maybe they get older, or feel they're successful enough – inevitably lose out. Leaders who inspire fear rather than respect are failures in my opinion. Hopefully that's something that contributes to low staff turnover, which is always good for your business, keeping hold of good people.

Now though, even with everything I have done so far, I still find I want to achieve more. I still enjoy pressure, I still enjoy new challenges – and maybe that is one of those essential characteristics that is part of being a success in business!

DOMINIC BURKE

People / Understand / Respect / Leader / Integrity

Dominic Burke started his career with a degree in politics and economics as a trainee account manager in a small insurance brokerage. Not long after, he took the risk, borrowed the money and took over the company through a management buyout. In 14 years he turned it into a region-leading insurance broker which boasted £16m revenues and had a staff of 230 people. While most people would proudly call it a success, his never-receding ambition led him to sell his firm to Jardine Lloyd Thompson. Six years on, Dominic found himself at the helm of the whole group, commanding the 4th largest global insurance broker – trading in 40 countries, with 11,000 staff and market capitalisation of £2bn. He is now even more driven than he was when he first started off. Here Dominic shares what he's learned along the way and what he thinks helps leaders jump over hurdles.

I was only 22 when I became a leader, which seems ridiculously young now. I was only the leader of 12 people at the time, admittedly, but it was my start. I did my degree at York, then came to work with my father at a small insurance firm called Berkeley Burke. He left and sold his part of the business not long after I joined – it might have been working with me that finished him off!

A few years later, I found myself borrowing money from a bank in Anfield in Liverpool, and leading a management buyout. It was my first business risk and I had to scrabble to make it happen – I had to go out on a limb.

Hindsight, all these years later, tells me I did the right thing but it wasn't that clear cut at the time. Liverpool in the 80s wasn't what it is today – the political and economic environment was completely different then. Nobody wanted to do business there. It was an uphill battle in that era, building up a small business when not much was happening at all in the city, but I genuinely think that uphill battle was part of what made me the man I am.

It helped me to develop a certain trading awareness, a certain 'nous' – commercial instincts that helped shape me and built me up for later challenges. Part of that is down to genetics, I think – a natural drive to take risk, to achieve, to push. But it's also education, opportunity, aspiration, a whole host of different parts which make up the nature versus nurture debate. In reality, of course, it is a combination of the two.

I genuinely also believe that there is such a thing as an environmental gene pool, not just parental. Certain places, Liverpool among them, seem to produce more than their average share of successful entrepreneurs – cities that are build on a history of trading, where people and their families going way back for generations have been involved in commerce. It all seems to contribute, to play a part in the make-up of the people who live there.

It's not necessarily to do with background in terms of wealth or privilege – a nurturing environment which supports individual achievement can be found in the humblest of homes. I think if you can successfully build a business in a challenging environment like Liverpool in the 80s, you can rule the world.

I got my first big break selling life assurance to Ford workers. I'd taken over the business after the buyout and was looking to develop it. I always had a real ambition to build it up, not just for myself but for the people who worked with me.

My uncle was a shop steward at the Ford plant, and he arranged for me to go in and make my pitch to them during their lunch break. I found myself standing in the refectory explaining all about it. In those days, none of them had cover like that and it was the real beginning for my company – Ford agreed to deduct the payments from wages, 10p a week to insure them and their wives. It wasn't easy, standing there in my early 20s flogging my products, but you have to be fearless. You have to lead with courage and with passion – no matter how small or how big your business. I'm proud of the fact that I still have that client today.

> Don't be afraid to be the only person in the room admitting you don't understand.

Being fearless shouldn't be confused with being reckless, though – there is a big difference. You have to believe in yourself and your decisions. At the same time, you have to make those decisions grounded in fact and commercial awareness – make sure you have all the facts, and that you understand them.

If there's one message I'd want to pass on to young entrepreneurs or those starting out in their careers, it's not to be afraid to say if you don't understand something. Don't be afraid to ask questions. Don't be afraid to be the only person in the room admitting you don't understand – you won't be, you'll just be the one brave enough to say so. It's absolutely vital to understand, to do your homework, because the better you understand, the more you know and the more confident you can be in your fearless decisions. I had a good education, but I'm by no means a genius. I work hard, I pay attention, and I'm loyal. You can't learn a lot of this stuff at university – apart from what they call the University of Life, of course.

Building up my business also allowed me to make my mistakes, to learn my lessons, and to use that commercial 'nous' that I still rely on now. By the year 2000, Burke Ford employed about 250 people in the UK, and was a much bigger concern than it was when we started. I was travelling up and down to London, developing the business, and I realised that I wanted to play on a bigger stage, which was the next big risk in my career. I felt confident and was sure I could be successful.

I did my research and approached Jardine Lloyd Thompson – they weren't a big US-owned firm, they were the cool underdog, which appealed to me as that's what I'd been. I didn't put the company up for sale, I just approached them to see if they wanted to acquire us. We became part of that group in 2000, and essentially I travelled upwards, becoming the CEO in 2005.

Obviously I'm now the leader of a much bigger company, and of many more people, but I still think some of the things you learn early on guide you later in life.

One thing you need to realise very soon is that honesty and integrity are important. You might get a certain way down the path of success without them, by being a bit too sharp for your own good, by playing games, but you will never rise to the top. In business, people don't have to like you – but they do need to respect you. If you are untrustworthy, shown up to be a liar, or don't display integrity in your business dealings, you will never truly succeed.

You can be clever, you can be smart, you can trade and you can push – but without honesty, integrity and transparency, it won't work as a whole. There's a subtle difference between being smart and being sharp. Even the smallest hints of dishonesty will hold you back. Cutting corners and trying to fool people will hold you back.

Many of us seem
to suffer from
a little bit of
insecurity – which
I mean in the
nicest possible
way, as that is
what inspires us to
constantly strive to
be better.

If you want to be a real leader, you have to walk a different path than that – one that inspires respect rather than distrust.

One of the most inspiring people I ever knew had a real skill for telling people things they might not want to hear in a way which made them appreciate hearing it. He could gather up information, and share that information, so well. Being able to present that in the right way, in a way that is smart and clever but also honest, influences people so much – it's a tremendous skill to have in business and in life; one of those that's partly instinct and partly experience.

Being able to manage people, to have them work not just for you but with you, is essential – if you want to lead, then people need to respect you. I've found over the years that the main way you earn that respect, the main way that people will want you to manage them and will trust you and admire you, is for you to be in the trenches with them.

You need to understand what they are facing, and be willing to face it with them – stand in the line of fire, defend your corner, fight the good fight. That's when people will respect your integrity and understand that you are in it with them. You're not just the boss, a toff, a distant figure in charge, but you are as invested in the goals of the business as they are. They also need to see your work ethic; I might be the CEO of a company that employs thousands of people, but I'm still usually the first person in the office in the morning. I still feel the need to be that involved.

I think that might actually be one of the common threads I've found in chief execs and other leaders who have achieved a certain level of success. Many of us seem to suffer from a little bit of insecurity – which I mean in the nicest possible way, as that is what inspires us to constantly strive to be better. There seems to be a fundamental urge to do better, to work harder, to prove yourself, to follow your ambitions. It's an internal motivating factor which seems to exist inside a lot of us. I can honestly say that I'm even more driven now than I was when I first started off.

Even outside work, that drive seems to kick in. Horse racing is a large part of my life and I'm now chairman of Newbury Racecourse. It feels like I'm still looking for hurdles to jump over – I know that at some point I'll need to be put out to grass, but I don't think it will be any time soon!

JUDY HALEWOOD

Business / Work / Winning / Success / People

Judy Halewood has led an interesting and adventurous life, with its fair share of challenges along the way. From the age of 12 she worked in the family flower shop, picking up business acumen which laid the foundation for later life. She was the first woman to breed, own and train a horse to compete in the world famous Grand National. Little did she realise that many years later she would become chairperson of Halewood International, the largest independent drinks manufacturer and distributor in the UK, sponsoring the same race with the first ever purse of £1m. She is also a breast cancer survivor, an experience which taught her important lessons in itself. Here Judy tells us about the similarities between the world of horse racing and the world of business, and about the importance of embracing the challenges life throws at us.

Horses have been part of my life from a very early age. Going back to my childhood, I spent most weekends riding, and that was my passion. I will never forget the snow-covered Christmas morning when my mother asked me to look in the garden at all the rabbits. I looked out of the window and there it was - a beautiful black Fell pony tied to a tree with a big red bow on it. It was the most wonderful sight I had ever seen and, wearing my dressing gown and slippers, I ran into the snow to meet my very first pony. That was when I became totally involved in the world of horses.

It might not seem like it to the casual observer, but the world of horses and racing has a lot in common with the world of business in which I later found myself involved.

From being the little girl riding my pony, I moved into the big world of horse racing. I loved everything about it. As a trainer, there is no better feeling than seeing your horse first past the post. To actually see your foal being born and then watch it winning a race is a magical experience. Your whole world revolves around that. But racing is all about winning. Second place just isn't good enough; winning is the ONLY thing that matters.

It's exactly the same in business. You start off with nothing, or with a small thing, an idea that has just been born, and you have to work at it until that idea turns into a successful business. You can't buy success and it doesn't happen over night. You need enough enthusiasm to eventually drive you to achieve bigger and better things, ensuring that it's your business which crosses the line first.

But horse racing wasn't the only way I learned about business when I was younger. I worked in the family flower shop from the age of 12, and my grandmother would often say 'your profit is on the floor'. She would then go and pick up any unused bits of greenery or flowers and make some little arrangement that she would sell for five shillings or whatever she could get. She was a wise lady, and the lesson not to waste anything in business stuck with me for the rest of my life.

Likewise, if I was given a chore to do that I wasn't happy about, my father used to say 'if a job needs doing, then do it to the best of your ability'. These simple lessons were instilled in me from a young age. If you have to do a job, you might as well do it with a smile on your face.

When I first started out in my own business as a horse trainer, I began at the bottom and slowly, with a lot of hard work, I built it up to the point where I started to win races. You have to work really hard to ensure your horse crosses that winning post first - but you can't always do it on your own. You have to have a dedicated team who will go on that journey with you. Similarly, to win in business you have to have a strong, motivated team around you as well. Each member adds their own individual talents to the overall group effort and it is very important to listen to, and respect, each member if you want to have a winning team in the industry full of fierce competition.

It's also important to accept that you will never be able to control everything in life. Challenges will always arise and you need to deal with them effectively.

There was a time in my horse racing career when I had to watch one of my horses being injured and later put down. That was horrendous. All that hard work and love for that animal, gone in one day. You start to doubt yourself and your capabilities. It's the same in business. No matter how hard you work, things go wrong at times and your business doesn't perform as well as you'd hoped. This is all part of the process. What's important is how you deal with the challenges and disappointments. You can't dwell on your failings but you must learn from them and move on.

When John Halewood, my partner and the founder of Halewood International, suddenly passed away, I found myself at the helm of a major company facing some tough decisions about how to carry on.

It was quite daunting at first, as I had never had to run a business of that size and scale. Even though I had been involved in the business, it's not the same as being the final decision-maker. It was a challenge to carry on with what John had created. I didn't want to fail him, but I had a lot of doubts about my capabilities. With hindsight, I realise that it was one of those occasions where you have to believe in yourself and just do your best.

Ultimately, after some soul-searching, I made the decision to continue John's legacy. The drinks industry is predominantly a male-orientated world and, as a woman, it was difficult at first to walk into the boardroom and deal with that, but I was the chairperson. I had to appear confident even if I felt a little intimidated at times. It was a great challenge to start with, but over the years it has become easier. I have learned a lot and it has made me a much stronger person.

My cancer journey also taught me a very valuable lesson.

When I was diagnosed, it was a huge shock to me as I lead a very healthy lifestyle. How could I possibly go through this and emerge at the other end? Would I survive at all? It was a time of great reflection and a huge learning curve. I can remember my nurse saying 'Judy, you've got to think of your treatment as climbing a ladder. You can't go from the first rung to the last in one go. You have to go one step at a time until you reach the top'.

> Sometimes you have to be out of your comfort zone and take risks that scare you, but it's the only way to progress in life and business.

This really helped me to get through the process. I did reach the top of that particular ladder and, thankfully, my health is good now. Surviving cancer put things into perspective for me. The principle of treating everything like a ladder is a good way to approach challenges in life and in business. We all want to get to the top as quickly as we can, and we get frustrated if the progress seems slow, but it is important to climb those individual rungs.

Quite often though, how fast things advance in business depends on the size of the risk or challenge you take on. Sometimes you have

You never know
what is round the
corner and you
can't always be
safe, but these are
the times that pro-
vide the best op-
portunities to learn
something new.

to be out of your comfort zone and take risks that scare you, but it's the only way to progress in life and business. In the last year alone, Halewood International has acquired Liverpool Gin and The Pogues Irish Whiskey, along with a significant share acquisition of West Cork Distillers. Buying another company or brand is always a risk, but you have to be prepared to take risks in order to reach new heights.

The Crabbie's Grand National was another major decision we took to create wider international brand awareness for Crabbie's, a number one selling alcoholic ginger beer in the UK. John had always had a dream of sponsoring The Grand National, so it was a very special moment when Halewood International finally did it, and in style - the Crabbie's Grand National came with the first £1m purse ever. John would have been so proud. He liked to dream big and make things happen. It's just so sad that he was never able to see it.

However, success usually comes at a cost. At times, maintaining the level of success your business is at can be very stressful, and it can be hard to have any down time. The rest of your life can take a back seat. Sometimes you don't sleep, you live and breathe your business. You are always thinking of how you can improve things. It can take its toll but the rewards of achieving your goals give you great pleasure.

> All of us have talents, it's just a matter of finding out what they are and focusing on them - and sometimes that happens during the most challenging of times.

It depends what you want out of life really. Some people are quite happy working 9 to 5, having a basic salary, going home and just switching off. They don't want the responsibility of owning a business or having the responsibility of other people working for them. There's nothing wrong with that. However, if you want to do really well, you have to be prepared to take work home with you every night.

Now, when I look back, I think very often people don't realise how capable they are. That applied to me too. Little did I know that, as that young girl working in the flower shop or riding my pony, I would end up being the chairperson of a major international company. Sometimes it's not until you're forced into a situation that you realise your strengths. All of us have talents, it's just a matter of finding out what they are and focusing on them - and sometimes that happens during the most challenging of times.

You never know what is round the corner and you can't always be safe, but these are the times that provide the best opportunities to learn something new. Sometimes you just have to do something that you don't think you can do, be a bit more adventurous. Even if you are uncomfortable, allow yourself to be uncomfortable for a while - you actually come out feeling better on the other side. Amazing things can happen and do happen. You just need to know what you want from life, keep focused on your goals and always look for the positives in everything. The rest will follow.

ROBERT HOUGH, CBE, DL

People / Opportunities / Passion / Luck / Leader

'You would be amazed how far you can travel if you try' - his own words perfectly describe the life of Robert Hough, a hugely respected business leader whose career has spanned the law, Peel Holdings, chairing vastly influential economic development agencies, and heading up Manchester's ground-breaking Commonwealth Games. His name has been associated with a total of 135 directorships over his lifetime. He is a Deputy Lieutenant of Greater Manchester and served as its High Sheriff in 2004. He was awarded the CBE for his services to business in the North West. Here Robert tells us why he is still passionate about business, and explains his unshakeable belief that the end game of improving the economy is, and should always be, about one thing – people.

I was always interested in business, from the very beginning of my career. As a solicitor, I specialised in corporate law and was fascinated by the way in which certain businesses would grow and thrive, and why that happened. To be honest, I still am fascinated by that. There is a particular combination of circumstances that invariably seem to contribute, for example, strategy, leadership, product, market and geography; and sometimes, perhaps, the less tangible element of good fortune.

I do think that luck is a factor. I view my involvement with Peel, which changed my whole career and ultimately my outlook on my goals and ambitions, as a fortuitous stroke of luck – or at least something that started that way.

John Whittaker, who founded Peel, was referred to the law firm where I worked in Manchester back in 1973, purely because of a conflict of interest with another firm. The fact that he walked through the door was pure luck – but the fact that I was willing to make the most of the opportunity was perhaps not. Those were very early days, but that event changed my whole life – I was the same person, but thanks to meeting and ultimately joining some years later the businesses of the inspirational John Whittaker and his companies, a whole different vista developed before me.

> You would be amazed how far you can travel if you try. You don't know what you're capable of until you stretch yourself to the limit.

That was lucky – but luck alone is never enough. I've noticed over the years that people who succeed in business are the people who are willing to say a resounding 'yes' to opportunities that come knocking. I, too, could so easily have stayed in my existing career in the law, and never made a move into the wider business world – and while saying 'yes' doesn't guarantee you will succeed, it does ensure you will at least have a chance.

I've always been the sort of person who says 'yes' to opportunities. I have always worked hard, put in maximum effort, done long hours. For anything I felt was worthy, I was willing to take on that responsibility, and make that commitment. Of course, that might take its toll in other areas of your life, such as with your family and home, which is a different consideration entirely.

But I do believe that you need to push yourself, to really go for it – you would be amazed how far you can travel if you try. You don't know what you're capable of until you stretch yourself to the limit.

The same is true when you face adversity. In business – in life – there will always be moments where you feel backed into a corner, in a thoroughly tight spot; where you feel like there is simply no way out of the difficulty you're in, whether it's a big problem you have created or a situation you were left with. The thing to remember is that there will be a way out – there always is. You just have to find it.

You need to be determined and persistent, and push and push and push. Think through the problem or the situation from all angles, probe and eventually you will find an opening. What feels insurmountable never is. Don't freeze – keep moving, keep active, keep searching for a solution.

And afterwards, once you've found the way out, learn from it – did you make a mistake? Could it have been avoided? What can you learn from it?

That kind of determination is something I've seen time and time again in successful business leaders. I have worked with some tremendous people, and I've definitely noticed those common qualities.

They are persistent. They work hard. They deal with setbacks, and see problems and challenges as part of their journey, rather than the end of it. They make what appear to be instinctive decisions with which they combine their hard work with self-belief. They can also multi-task to a huge degree, juggling complex issues, situations and ideas in their minds.

Most of the time, they also combine less measurable qualities – such as vision, instinct, self-belief, charisma – with sheer effort, determination, and really knowing their business inside-out. But nobody makes it in business on their own, and nobody makes it without the ability to be a strong leader.

They also know how to spot an opportunity first and they are never afraid to close a deal, even though it may cost a little more than expected in the first instance. They also recognise how strength in one's market, and holding prize assets in the broadest sense, really does matter.

Strong leaders acknowledge their own qualities and weaknesses; they also understand the strengths and weaknesses of the people they work with, and they are not afraid to say when they have made a mistake. Strong leaders have integrity and standards, which inspire people to believe in them and follow them.

Now, I think, more than ever, that integrity and personal reputation is important. We live in a highly competitive world, and very often your unique offering will be that reputation. If you are looking for funders or partners or new customers, your reputation and that of your company will be priceless – and incredibly hard to repair once damaged. These potential collaborators won't just be assessing your finances – they will be assessing you, the way you work, and your trustworthiness.

Sometimes, I think, you only see the true worth of a leader when times are tough. It's easy to lead when everything is going well, when everything is easy. It's when people are in challenging situations, when things are going wrong, that you see their true worth – when a leader can remain strong and positive and inspirational even in the most difficult of circumstances. That's important in a downturn when the challenge is always that you do not know when it will stop getting worse. If a leader can get you through a steep recession, when the economy takes a severe downward turn, he or she can get you through about anything.

Conversely, there are examples I've seen over the years where people have failed. Partly, it's from not having the skills I've just described, but sometimes there are other issues. A business needs not just a good product and plan, but also strong foundations – if you are ambitious, and want to build something of size and scale, you need to have the internal structures that will support your expansion, or your plans. You need processes that work, and you need a good and loyal team to work them.

Being passionate purely about making money doesn't tend to work for most people in the long term.

The days of making a deal on the back of a fag packet are gone – you need to have your systems in place. You need to be able to combine your passion and flair with a solid team or structure that supports your work, or eventually it may come tumbling down.

Equally, it is vital in today's world to be collaborative, to understand the big goal and to forge partnerships, and also to have the drive and diplomacy to create strong relationships across a broad spectrum.

I think finding something you are passionate about is also essential. Being passionate purely about making money doesn't tend to work for most people in the long term. Successful business people tend to deliver something special, something with extra value – and that extra value often comes from their passion.

I have also realised that any success I may have achieved has been crucially dependent on the support and encouragement I have had from my wife and family (and years ago, my parents) and also from my work colleagues, especially my secretary of 23 years.

For me, it's been an evolution. When I started my legal career, I wasn't thinking about what good I could do in the world. I was largely thinking I had a good job in which I was interested and which would allow me to progress in my career.

It was only later in life, as I started to grasp hold of some of those opportunities that came my way, that I started to see a very different side of business and the benefits it brings.

A big turning point came when I was deeply involved in the 2002 Commonwealth Games in Manchester. That was a ground-breaking affair, in that it changed the way we drew benefit from these huge sporting events. For the first time, it wasn't just about the sport – it was about using the opportunity as a tool for regeneration in a part of the city that badly needed it.

The Games, enabled by the strategic vision of Manchester City Council, revitalised and left a rich legacy for the whole East Manchester area, in a way that had never been done before, but has since been replicated with the London 2012 Olympics, and in other parts of the world.

It was a complete eye-opener as far as I was concerned – seeing the way that people's lives, whole communities, would be changed by the economic, social and environmental impact of the Games.

Since then, I've been involved with various organisations that aim to develop the economy of the region, such as chair of the North West Development Agency and New East Manchester and, latterly, the Liverpool City Region Local Enterprise Partnership, all great organisations that have made significant contributions through acute knowledge and collaborative partnerships, for economic growth and social improvement in their respective areas. I simply couldn't be prouder of the way the North West has progressed, the way it has made the most of its natural assets, developed new ones, and turned a corner for a future of great new opportunity.

There has been an explosion of confidence, of ambition, of delivery, that actually makes me tingle. It is so exciting to see what has been achieved, and what more lies ahead.

This aspect of my work has become extremely important to me – the realisation that the end game of improving the economy, of driving investment, of supporting business, is all about people.

Everything is about people. It's about improving the quality of life of all who live here, about raising aspirations and creating opportunities for everyone – that might be for entrepreneurs, it might be for people who simply want a good job and the chance to achieve in life, or it might be for a school leaver looking for training or an apprenticeship or career guidance.

For me, now, business is inextricably tied up with those people. A successful business by what it does can help attack social inequality, it can improve skills and training, it can boost social wellbeing at every level and deliver economic regeneration. Business is not just about money – it is also about changing the world we live in for the better.

I'd be untruthful if I said I viewed it that way when I was starting out in my career. I didn't have an especially over-developed sense of social justice – but finding that passion and working with outside agencies and local authorities has opened up for me a whole new aspect of the benefit of business for me.

This summer, I am going back to Peel, and will be concentrating on developing its regional airports. It feels a little like going home – back to the company which whisked me away from the law, and gave me so many opportunities.

But this time, I will be going back with the benefit of not only passion and belief, but a lifetime of skills and experience under my belt. I feel that my knowledge and my drive and my energy remain undiminished. I'll still be looking for opportunities to grasp, and ways to make a difference.

SIR MICHAEL BIBBY

People / Risk / Values / Trust / Money

The Bibby Line Group is one of the most historic and well known names in global shipping – but changing markets, and the need to constantly adapt to a business world in a state of flux, have resulted in a company that is not only involved in shipping but in offshore oil and gas services, retail, distribution, financial services and memorial parks. From its 19th century roots, it has grown into a £1.7bn company that employs more than 6,000 people and operates in 20 countries. Sir Michael Bibby, MD of the group and the sixth generation of Bibbys at the helm, shares his views on the need to adapt and diversify; the importance of strong values, and not falling into the trap of thinking you know everything!

Bibby Line Group might be a family firm, but there was no assumption that I would be following in my father's footsteps and joining it. I have three brothers and a sister and, in fact, I'm the only one who joined the executive. My dad had two simple rules about it: we had to be good enough and, perhaps more importantly, we really had to want to do it.

It's that deep-seated motivation – the wanting to do it – that is absolutely vital if you are going to make a success of business. Whether you're working for someone else, or starting your own enterprise, you need that motivation. You have to want it badly, and be willing to really work for it. You need to know what you want, and have the intelligence, the 'nouse', whatever you want to call it, to make it happen.

Before I came in to Bibby, I qualified as a chartered accountant with a London firm, and I went to work for Unilever. I was there for several years as a project accountant, and gained some fantastic experience. That was important – as I said, there was no hard and fast rule that I would join the company. I could have stayed at Unilever, or gone elsewhere. It was also useful in that it allowed me to prove myself because, while having the opportunity to join a family firm is a privileged position, it is also important that the people who work with you know that you didn't just get the job because of your surname. I had to establish that I was up to it.

The company has grown a great deal since I joined, so I have to assume we have got more right than wrong to date. We've taken risks, diversified, and mostly it has paid off. Don't get me wrong, there has been a fair share of mistakes, there always are. Risk, by its nature, does not always go the way you want it to – and everyone makes mistakes. All you can do in those situations is look, learn, and move on. For someone who runs a business that's more than 200 years old, I don't actually do a lot of looking back – I like to keep going forward. If something fails, you see what lessons you can learn, and then don't dwell on it too much or it will affect your confidence and your future decision making.

Risk is a vital part of business. It might be wanting to move into a new sector, or investing in a new idea, or deciding how many eggs to put in each basket. In each situation, you have to ask yourself certain questions, and you have to gather as much information as you can. We, for example, at Bibby, would do all the usual stuff – analysis of the market, the competition, return on capital, modelling, etc. We also look at the strategic aspect – how does this risk fit in with our company's values? Does it play to our strengths? Are we looking at this as a short-term investment for a quick win, or a longer term project? I can't do all of this on my own. We have a team I trust who work together on it all. Armed with this information, this analysis, and your own instincts, you will eventually decide whether the risk is worth it or not.

With us, diversification has been the key. It's the reason why Bibby Line is the only Liverpool shipping line left owning and managing deep sea ships in the city. Up until about 1960, the bulk of our work was based on ships moving troops around and on the UK to Burma trade route. After that, things started to change – air travel became much more common and the Burma trade dried up.

The end of the Empire and changing methods of transport affected everyone, and most big shipping companies in the city went bankrupt. We didn't, and the reason why was that we changed, and we adapted – and we have to continue to do that today. It is the way that all businesses have to be these days – I don't think it's even a choice any more. The world, and business, moves at a very fast pace – communications, knowledge, customer choice –and you need to adapt to survive.

Having a diversified portfolio of businesses acts as a way of offsetting risk to some extent – the different parts are something like separate portions of a share portfolio and exposure to different markets, regions and people means it is less likely that any one event can affect all your activities. In any business, I think, if you don't realise this, and you're not willing to change and adapt to the market or the needs of your customers, you'll be tripped up at some point or another.

It's easy to fall
into the trap of
thinking you know
everything but,
in reality, nobody
does. Nobody is
that good!

For me, one of the ways I manage to make solid decisions, balance risks, and keep moving forward, is by having a good team around me. That old saying about always employing people who are better than you definitely holds true. At Bibby, we try and keep office politics to a minimum and simply find people who are good at what they do, who will get on with the job and, perhaps most importantly, are trustworthy. The bigger your business gets, the more you will need to delegate, which makes that trust even more vital.

It's easy to fall into the trap of thinking you know everything but, in reality, nobody does. Nobody is that good! You have to be able to rely on other people. There will always be people out there whose skills and expertise complement your own, and finding them is an essential part of success. Even if you're born with the best set of business genes in the world, it's also a case of how you use them – and I'd suggest that a sensible way to use those instincts you might naturally have is by finding great people to help you along the way. Liverpool is a far more attractive proposition now than it used to be. It's considered a good place to live and work, a credible business base. More needs to be done, but these days you can attract good professional candidates to move here and stay here.

As well as being able to choose that team, I'd say that you also need to be a bit of a chameleon. Obviously, this isn't something you learn at university, but it's vital. You want to make something happen, so the people who work with you need to want it too. You have to be able to motivate them, to get them to buy in to it. To do that, you need to understand them – some people will respond better to an emotional approach, some are completely rational, others prefer financial or strategic reasoning. Some situations call for a kind of benign dictatorship, in others you need to be highly consultative.

I'd say that I have to use that chameleon behaviour every day in business – if you want to get your message across, you need to understand what people will respond to. You also have a responsibility to the people who work with you. In my case, that's more than 6,000 employees. I'd be lying if I said that responsibility doesn't sometimes feel like a burden, but there is a flip side.

Nothing makes you feel better than seeing someone who is good at their job come up through the company, seeing them make a success of their careers and knowing that you've had such a positive impact on their lives and those of their family. On a lot of occasions, they have just as much emotional investment and pride in Bibby as members of the direct family.

For us, there is another equally important aspect to our business. We have a well-developed set of company values, and we reflect those across all of our different interests. One of the most important questions we ask when looking at something new, or making a big decision, is does it fit with our values? Does it fit with what we're all about, with what we stand for?

Obviously we're a business and we want to make money – but the values are incredibly meaningful to us. They're built on qualities such as trust, innovation, working together, being better and, quite simply, doing the right thing. Since 2007, Bibby Line Group employees have also donated more than £8.4 million to over 1,000 charitable causes.

CSR is sometimes perceived as a box to be ticked but, for us, it's an essential part of what we do – and it's also something that our employees find very special. They get a great deal of satisfaction from being involved, helping to raise money for causes they believe in. It's a real unifying factor for the extended Bibby family. Yes, making money is important – but it's not everything.

For me, as the sixth generation of Bibbys, I am also looking forward to building a bigger, stronger, even more resilient business for future generations. I don't like to use the word 'legacy', as it implies a lot of negative pressure. I don't see it like that – I genuinely enjoy the experience, I enjoy my work, and, I'd say again, you need to feel that sense of enthusiasm for business to succeed in it. If you don't feel energised and inspired, that will be reflected throughout the organisation.

Having said all that, perhaps if I could offer some advice on balancing life and work, it would be to make sure you can switch off! I'm lucky that I can, I've always been able to disconnect my brain from business worries and sleep well at night. You need to find a way to do that which works for you – switch off your phone, charge things up where you can't hear them, and don't live your life glued to your iPad!

GEORGE DOWNING

People / Money / Ambitious / Instincts / Keep it simple

His father used to tell him that he had to eat, sleep and drink business if he wanted to succeed. Those were the teenage days, when families with two cars seemed really posh and the £10,000 he made from selling his share in a snooker club felt like an absolute fortune. Decades later, George Downing is referred to as a property magnate with £1b worth of completed developments, iconic buildings in his portfolio and never receding business ambitions. Having retained his unpretentious character, George reflects on what skills and attributes he thinks helped him get there, and what aspiring entrepreneurs should focus on as they also strive to succeed.

I've always been a really ambitious person. Some of that came from my dad – he was old school, a real larger-than-life character. We used to talk about life and business and ambitions all the time. He used to tell me I needed to eat, sleep and drink business if I wanted to make it work.

When you're younger, some dreams seem really hard to pursue. I remember going round to my mates' houses when I was a kid and seeing they had two cars – to me, that meant they were really posh. I know now it didn't, but I can still remember that feeling like it was yesterday.

I was able to use motivations like that, and the advice my dad gave me, and combine it with my own ambition. I wanted to achieve something, I wanted to succeed – but even back then, I didn't want to be greedy.

There's a fine line, really, between being ambitious and being greedy, and it can catch people out. I've seen it happen. Greed can poison people whereas ambition can drive them on to be better at what they are doing. Business for me is about finding your product, your market, and being the best in class – it's not just about money.

It's important to know the difference between the two, and be educated by it. Being greedy sometimes means you don't know when to switch off, to back off, to stop. Being greedy might get you short term gain, but longer term it often leads to failure. If you try and run before you can walk, it won't end well.

I was running the snooker club by the time I was 18, but always knew I wanted to do more. In my 20s someone bought me out for £10,000. That was in the 1980s and it seemed like an absolute fortune to me.

It gave me an opportunity, one I decided to take. I started off buying property then – I'd never been able to figure out why terraced houses in Liverpool were so cheap. I thought it'd be a good idea to buy some and use them for student accommodation. That was in the early days of it all really, but even then I developed some rules – guidelines I suppose – that helped me.

Firstly, again, being ambitious but not greedy. Secondly, don't get knocked off your path, especially when you're just starting out. You might be unsure, but don't let it dampen your ambitions. Thirdly, keep it simple.

That sounds a bit daft, 'keep it simple', but it still applies now. It's about being sensible but also trusting your instincts. Use your common sense. Don't run before you can walk, no matter how keen you are. Yes, you have to take risks - but you have to prepare for them, try and make the right decisions. Being ambitious isn't the same as being reckless. The flip side of that is that you also have to sometimes trust yourself and make gut decisions. As you go along, your experience and your instincts develop and work better together.

Back in those early days, I was a lad in my 20s and I was buying and doing up houses. I was keeping it simple: buying as many as I could in one street, so there were more students in there, and it created a sense of community.

That was good business, but it also kept it simple. I was really determined to build my business, but I wasn't ignoring quality – I did the houses up nicely, I spent a bit of money on them, it improved the look and feel of the whole street. Because of that, the other residents didn't view the student houses as problems and if there were any problems, I would go along in person, knock on their door, and apologise and try and sort it out. Try and treat people the way you'd want to be treated.

These days I'm sometimes described as a property magnate – but owning a business like Downing doesn't happen overnight, or by accident. It started with those few houses on a few streets, and was built on ambition, hard work, and a little bit of luck.

I do feel I've been lucky – I know we all get luck, good and bad, but I definitely feel that in those early days I was a little bit of a chancer who got a few breaks. Sometimes I look back now and realise how lucky I was. I always had self-belief and ambition, I always believed I could build something and achieve something, but at the same time I was always very self-critical. I felt like I was winging it, flying by the seat of my pants! I'd had no formal training and was probably the worst pupil at my school – I just wasn't academic and had report cards full of 'could try harder'.

But in business, I did try harder – I really pushed it. My goal – my initial aim – was to have 50 tenants. I thought if I could get those 50 tenants, I could pay the mortgage off and I'd be made. I know lots of business people constantly set goals but in all honesty, that was the only one I ever set. And I exceeded it.

I suppose the first really big project I did was the old Maternity Hospital on Oxford Street in Liverpool. My son was born there and when I was visiting, the midwife mentioned that it was going up for sale. I remember leaving, after my visit with the baby, and thinking on the way out: look how big this place is - I could really do something here.

> There's nothing wrong with working hard to earn more money, it's when it takes over from everything else that the problems start.

In between the terraced houses, I'd worked on student accommodation on Mount Pleasant, so it wasn't just a giant leap from one to the other – but it took a bit of nerve. In the end, I pulled it off – it was my first big student deal. I had students in there, young doctors and nurses to start off with, and it was high quality so I was able to charge more. It was one of those situations where I had to balance the risk with the ambition, and decide whether it was worth it.

In that case, it was. It was the start of it all to some extent – my first big deal.

Even now, though, I still see the same things I admire in business people, and the same things I know will eventually trip them up.

It's back to greed again; it's not all about money, and pursuing just money won't work. I've seen people with great business ideas fail because they've taken their eye off the ball – got distracted by success, or money, and lost their concentration. Wanting more is a natural human instinct, and there's nothing wrong with working hard to earn more money, it's when it takes over from everything else that the problems start.

I look back at 2007, and the big recession then. People were caught out and I saw a lot of people suffer, and it reinforced some of the beliefs I'd always had: keep it simple. Don't be greedy. Don't over-trade. Don't spend more money than you can afford to. Don't fall into the trap of borrowing too much just because you can. Time and time again I see people failing because of poor management of finances and projects, not the actual idea or concept.

If I'd gone nuts in those early days, when I was buying my first few houses, and started spending all my profits on luxuries, I'd never have had enough to progress any further. Making money is one thing, keeping it is another entirely. It's a basic rule of household budgeting: always keep a few bob tucked away!

Everyone goes through tough times in business. Times when you're working crazy hours and you feel like you're making a lot of sacrifices. Times when it's easier to see why you're doing it than others. 2007, again, was a hard time – an eye opener. It didn't make me doubt what I was doing, but it did make me value even more those basic rules.

In honesty, I was lucky again. I'd sold off a chunk of property just before it all crashed down – and it's not as though I was some financial guru who predicted it all, I wasn't. I was just made a good offer and a good price and I took it, which meant I had enough to tide me over the hard times, and in fact go on to have a really good year.

But when those times do come – which they will – it's again about keeping your eye on the ball. Don't bury your head in the sand. If, for example, you're on a construction job and it's costing too much, you can't ignore that or hope for the best. You have to keep a close

Making money is
one thing, keeping
it is another
entirely.

eye on it, face up to it, make some hard decisions on what risk is worth it and what risk isn't. Sometimes you might need to take that risk, other times you might decide you can't spend money you don't have, but the one thing you can't do is ignore it.

When I was younger, I listened to advice a lot less than I do now. It was all part of that 'winging it' phase. I was really driven, really ambitious, but even then I was conscious of the fact that I wasn't paying enough interest to what the professionals were telling me. I knew I was probably doing things wrong, but I carried on anyway.

As you get older, as your business develops, as you have more money and your projects get bigger and everything expands, then you have the luxury of not having to wing it on your own anymore! In some ways it's more challenging – you have more responsibilities – but in some ways, it's less scary! I really value, now, the people I have around me – choosing good teams to work with, good professionals to listen to. I've learned so much from them, from the accountants and the developers and the architects and everyone else I've worked with.

Having more money, and more security in your business, also means you can be even fairer with people. I always tried to be straight and fair, especially financially, even in the early days – but as time goes on, the fairer you can be, and the more you can appreciate other people's talents and skills. I still find working a joy: coming in, being with people who work hard for me and with me, people who are also ambitious and who can share the fruits of our mutual labour. I don't think I could ever retire. I don't have enough hobbies to keep me busy, apart from anything else!

I think also, though, as you get older, you realise how much satisfaction there is to be taken from things that can't be measured purely in profit. In the early days, that's important, and of course it still is – but there is huge satisfaction in knowing I've made a difference through my work. Even early on, doing up a few houses in Kensington made a difference. The student homes I did on Mount Pleasant were buildings that had been derelict for ages.

Now, when I walk up Hardman Street and up to where our offices are, I see how different it all is. I've been part of the regeneration of Liverpool, and other cities, and it is really satisfying.

That is something that money can't buy – working hard, doing a good job, fulfilling your ambitions. It's something that all young people should be encouraged to do. They need to aspire to greatness, or to be the best that they can be. You see so many really bright young people wasted. They sometimes turn their skills and their determination towards something negative, instead of using all that focus and ingenuity on something legitimate and positive.

Everyone, whether they are entrepreneurs or not, should be ambitious. You might start off as a shelf-stacker in a supermarket, but you have to believe you could end up as the next Terry Leahy. Being ambitious is about being the best you can be – working as hard as you can, doing the best job, striving to achieve. That applies whether you are working for someone else or running your own business. Being an employee doesn't mean you've failed; you can still be ambitious no matter what you are doing. Not everyone wants to run their own business and being realistic in your ambitions means you can still go on to great things.

Young people need encouragement and support – but they also need to be able to look in the mirror, and say 'am I really doing the best I can? Am I keeping it real? Am I pushing myself?' Asking those questions applies whether you are an entrepreneur, or starting a new job, or already established in your career. It's about making things happen, no matter what your work environment is.

I meet people sometimes and they tell me they are ambitious, but when you push them and try and find out what they are ambitious for, it's really just about wanting more money. There's nothing wrong with wanting more money, but it's important not to confuse greed and ambition. You need to be willing to put in the hard graft, the hours, the effort. It's like that old saying: the more you practice, the luckier you get!

Without being willing to put in that hard graft, to push yourself, then it's an unrealistic ambition – like wanting to play for Everton without being bothered going to training. Be ambitious, yes, but also keep it real. Focus. Keep it simple – and always try to exceed your own expectations.

JENNY STEWART

People / Fail / Fears / Different / Believe

Jenny Stewart's career has spanned the Diplomatic Service, the Foreign and Commonwealth Office, director-level posts in the private sector and running her own businesses. Since 2012, she has been Chief Executive Officer of the Liverpool Chamber, helping to create and support business, and encouraging global trade. It also delivers the National Apprenticeship Service, creating more than 300 new jobs each year for young people, and Spark Up, which works with emerging entrepreneurs. Here she talks about the importance of facing your fears, building a personal brand, and why early failure can lead to later success.

Business, and life, is full of things that we are scared of. Things that make us feel uncomfortable. I'm not necessarily just talking about a fear of heights, or spiders, or whatever it is — but all kinds of personal fears.

That could be the fear of certain situations in a workplace, for example talking to an employee about a problematic sickness record. Or taking risk. Public speaking or presenting. Or planning. It will be different for everyone, but one thing I've noticed successful entrepreneurs have in common is facing those fears. They have become comfortable with being uncomfortable.

They have faced their fears and found ways to deal with them. We can all do that, if we get into good habits — do one thing every day that scares you. Learn to relax through the situation, become familiar with your own reactions. All of this will help you to be stronger. Some people seem to just exude confidence, but I can guarantee that even the most successful person in the world still has to take a deep gulp in certain situations! They're still able to carry on, to appear so confident, even if they are faking it, because they know and understand their own fears.

Knowing your own strengths and weaknesses is absolutely essential in business. Again, the most successful business person on the planet simply can't be good at everything, even if they come across that way — it's not possible. The key is to figure out which parts of a plan you are brilliant at, and which parts will require a little extra help.

> It's not the failure that matters, it's what you take from it, and how you move on.

Understand where you will need that help, and don't be afraid to ask for it. It takes confidence to admit you need help, but you won't survive without it. No man is an island. The same goes with mentoring — even if you don't have a formal mentor or coach, reach out to people. Find people you trust, from different walks of life or business, who will

You can't expect
other people
to believe in
you if you
don't appear
to believe in
yourself.

be honest with you and give you solid advice. Sometimes you simply need to be told to stop moaning, or to get on with it – but sometimes you need a fresh perspective, or for them to recognise that you have a problem, and perhaps suggest different ways of solving it.

I still have mentors, several of them. I think you always need to be open to listening to other people, even if sometimes you don't want to! Everyone will have a slightly different take on a situation or an issue, and although you might not always agree with them, it can help you develop your own view and your own resolve.

A big fear, for a lot of people, is failure. We don't like failure in this country, and that makes people nervous, possibly puts them off even trying in some situations. I genuinely believe that failure is an essential part of learning in business. It will happen to everyone at some point, there's no getting away from it – there will be a mistake, or something simply won't work out the way you expected.

I've found that entrepreneurs who have those failures early on in their careers always end up being more successful in the long term. Failing is a way to learn, if you let it be – and if you do it nearer the beginning, you can fail quickly, fail cheaply and fail efficiently! That said, I have also seen people who seem doomed to repeating the same mistakes over and over again. It's not the failure that matters, it's what you take from it, and how you move on.

One of the other common factors I've seen in people who make their businesses work is the effort they've put into building their personal brand. They appear self-confident, even if they don't always feel it, because you can't expect other people to believe in you if you don't appear to believe in yourself.

They have integrity, which is a quality people respond to. You can have everything in the world, but without integrity, it means nothing. Integrity is about being true to yourself, and true to the people around you. It's about learning that if something doesn't feel right, it probably isn't – trusting your own gut, and having the strength to follow what your instincts tell you.

People with integrity come across as reliable, trustworthy, dependable. These are all things you want to be in business. Deliver what you promise, exceed expectations, show that you are a good person to be in business with – offering a value for money product, service or experience isn't just about being the cheapest. It's about relationships.

Relationships are at the heart of business. Whether it's a relationship with a member of staff, or a client, or someone you meet at a networking event, it matters. Building good relationships is what it's all about. I advise people to always make eye contact, smile, treat people well. My mother raised me to believe we are all equal, whether that is people in far worse situations than you, or people far above you in the pecking order. We are all human beings and deserve to be shown respect.

So don't just go to an event, and give someone your business card, and magically expect the world to be your oyster – work on those relationships. Be likeable. Get out there. Be aware of what your competitors are offering, and find ways to make what you are offering more attractive. Sometimes that can simply be the way you present yourself, the way you interact, the first impression you make.

That is essential in business, but it's also applicable in many different situations. The attributes that will make you a successful business person will also get you noticed in the workplace: energy, passion, motivation, reliability, wanting to make an impact. People talk about skills all the time, but in my opinion a real education includes developing these attributes – preparing you for life, not just how to pass a test.

Being motivated, wanting to make an impact, are key factors in business success. I've seen entrepreneurs fall into two main categories: those who are in love with the idea of themselves becoming someone, and those who are in love with an idea or a concept or an invention that they believe can make a real difference in the world.

The first type often fail, as they don't know how to make what they want to happen actually happen – they're sold on the idea of being the next Richard Branson, but aren't really sure how to do it. The second type understand that the right product or service is the key, and that the rest will follow.

They may not be the only person providing that product or service, though, and that's where all those personal life skills come in – the ones that make a huge difference.

One of the big ones is communication. In fact, I'd say it's the single most important aspect of succeeding in business. You need to be able to communicate well with your customers or potential customers, your staff, your partners, you backers, your networks – there is a big, wide world out there, and a huge variety of ways to communicate.

Communication has changed more in the last 60 months than in the last 60 years, and we all need to be aware of it. It's so easy to tweet, to press send on an email, to publish something online. There are huge benefits – but also huge potential dangers. We all need to think a little harder about how we communicate, the messages we send out and the way we send them.

Those messages aren't always sent out in a straightforward fashion. Sometimes we might not even be aware of the fact that we're sending a message at all, because the other side of the equation is the way other people perceive us. Perception is the flipside of our communications and there are so many subtle ways to influence that, for good and for bad. Being aware of the way we come across, the look and feel of how our image is reflected and perceived, is something we need to be very careful with. It all goes back to that concept of building your personal brand.

It probably sounds, to a young entrepreneur starting out in life, like there is way too much to remember. Too much to manage, and think about, in addition to all the usual stresses of starting a business.

This is where forming those good habits comes in again, as well as being aware of your own strengths and weaknesses. Take time management as an example – some people just seem to have more hours in the day than others. Some people, though, seem to be constantly saying 'I didn't have time to do that,', or 'I was too tired.'

There are ways around this. Get into better habits, better routines. You need to have a bigger picture – a vision – but you also need to be aware of the way you are going to make it happen; the steps you need to take to get you where you want to go.

Make a plan, no matter how boring that might sound. Where do you see yourself in five years? What goals do you need to achieve to get there? Within each of those goals, what are the specific actions and steps required? Be strict with yourself. Don't let yourself meander, lose time, lose focus, get distracted. Having a plan will help you with that, even though it doesn't sound like a very exciting idea.

The fact is that in this country, 85% of businesses will fail within three years. That's a hard statistic to face, and it's not something that everyone is cut out to do. But by getting yourself into those good habits – facing your fears, building your personal skills, getting the support you need, recognising your good and bad points, being aware of what image you are potentially projecting – there are ways you can definitely increase the odds in your favour.

MICHAEL OGLESBY, CBE, DL

People / Family / Cash / Profit / Relationship

Michael Oglesby is living proof that you don't need a grand plan to succeed in life. Leaving school at just 16, he started his career as an apprentice in his father's heating and plumbing firm because he didn't really know what else to do. But a few decades later, he went on to found the Bruntwood Group, a leading commercial property company with a portfolio worth more than £900m and a revenue of more than £100m. Along the way he was named as a Businessman of the Year by the CBI and received a CBE for his services to charity. Here he tells us about the lessons learned from early business failures, the importance of doing the right thing and why you can never take your eye off the ball when it comes to cash flow.

I can't say that I ever had a grand plan for my life, and certainly not in my early years. I didn't do spectacularly well at school and had no real idea what I wanted to do for a career – so I ended up as an apprentice in my father's heating and plumbing firm, for lack of better ideas.

Although I quite obviously didn't remain a plumber for long, there was definitely something about those early days, the environment I was raised in and working with hands-on a building site which had a real effect on me. We lived above the shop and both my parents worked in the business. They worked long, hard hours, but they both enjoyed it, and it certainly provided a living for them and their family. Perhaps because of this early influence, it did feel natural to me to start my own business.

> Starting a business, though, is just that – a start. It's sustaining it that matters.

Starting a business, though, is just that – a start. It's sustaining it that matters – making sure it survives. My first venture was launched when I was just 22, after I'd got a degree in Building from what became Aston University. It lasted 10 years, and was quite successful but, to cut a long story short, I became involved in some big housing projects that were eventually our undoing.

The business went under and that was an extremely tough time in my life. I felt as though I had let everyone down – my family, my employees, the sub-contractors, everyone who was involved with the business in the wider community. I felt like I'd had a moral obligation to them and that it had all gone horribly wrong. It felt like the end of the world at the time, so much so that I knew I needed a fresh start.

I packed up my family and we moved, eventually to the North West, to start again. My sense of failure was so extreme at the time that I thought moving away was the only option, to completely build up from the ground somewhere new. That in itself wasn't easy. My wife and family moved around with me and we lived in five different houses in one year. Without her support, things could have been very different.

It's easy to say, with hindsight, that it was all part of the journey, that I learned lessons from it that helped me later in my business career. And that would be true – but of course it didn't feel like that at the time. It was awful; when you are in the thick of a situation like that it can be hard to see a way out. You are beset with doubts and anxieties and aren't always seeing the bigger picture.

But I did learn from it, a huge amount – and I never gave up on myself. I still was confident that I could succeed at something.

The main lesson I took away from the experience was the importance of cash flow. Don't get carried away with the sides of the business you enjoy – which for me, was getting out and about building things – but know all of your business, inside out. Always stay in control of your finances, and be aware of the need for cash.

Cash is what makes the difference when times get tough. Bruntwood has weathered several severe economic storms, and that is why. We have always made a profit, always had our cash flow in order. You have to understand every aspect of your business, especially the finances – it is too important to simply be handed over to someone else.

Sustainability and survival are the key words for me. And that all-round knowledge of your business is what helps you achieve those goals, it's not only about ideas and deals and projects. Yes, of course you need to take risk, but you also need to be cautious. It is a strange combination of dreaming big but also being a realist – a mix of instinct and sound financial reasoning. No matter how exciting an opportunity might seem, never take your eye off the numbers.

Bruntwood has always made a profit – these days that might seem old-fashioned, and a lot of businesses seem to survive on volume rather than profit. But for me, it's essential – without profit, without cash flow, ultimately your business will die. You can play clever games and dress your balance sheet but, if you run out of money, it's basically game over.

When Bruntwood was founded in the 1970s we had very little money, and it was a very challenging economic climate. It is almost certain that we are heading into yet another challenging climate right now. But the key is to stay calm, and remember that times like these can also offer opportunities – for people who are brave, there isn't a better time to start a business!

I can, of course, say that because I am looking back over my career, but I think it's true. I also think that in hard times, other things come into play. Your reputation is absolutely paramount in business – because business is all about people.

It's about your employees to start with. Employ good people, train them, look after them. If you build that kind of relationship – one based on mutual trust – you will be able to rely on them when things are hard. You can't expect to give the whole 'times are tough, we need to pull together' speech if you haven't made them feel part of a team and an essential part of the company.

Your relationship with your customers is absolutely vital. You need to have an awareness of changing markets and circumstances, to anticipate their needs, to respond to what they want. You need to be generating your own ideas, projects, income, all based on those relationships. Nobody is going to give you a good relationship with your customers – it's up to you to create it.

Then, there is your relationship with the wider community. We have always felt this is important for a variety of reasons. We do a lot of work within our communities, with less well off areas, in the arts and in philanthropy generally. Those are ties that bind in the best possible way – and it's important to do the right thing, to set your values and live by them. If the community in which you work does not function properly, then your business will not function properly and be successful.

Doing the right thing, in terms of supporting communities and getting involved in the places where you operate, is satisfying. It has moral value. But it also, as a pleasant side effect, genuinely has busi-

Starting a business isn't like having a job. It's not just time-consuming or hard work, it is a way of life.

ness value – people see what you are doing, and respect that. People, on the whole, want to do business with people they like and admire and respect.

Being true to your word, having those moral values, is all part of long-term sustainability and survival. If you want to be the kind of person who looks to take unfair advantage over others, who wants to take every last drop of profit from a situation, you will ultimately lose out. Of course, you might have some short term gains – but eventually nobody will want to work with you. Your customers and your colleagues won't trust you.

You will have lost your reputation – which might be an intangible concept, but has very tangible results. We all want to be treated fairly in life, but that means you have to be fair with others as well. Your standing in both the business and wider community is essential to your future, so value it – doing the right thing is a win-win!

Of course, you could say that I am giving this advice with the benefit of hindsight, and of course I am. It's harder to identify regrets when everything has, ultimately, turned out well.

If there is one thing I would say, it is to work at the balance between career and family. That's an extremely hard balance to strike. I was by no means a bad father, but I missed too many rugby games when my son was playing, and was absent at times when I should have been present.

Getting that balance right is important – not only for your family, but for you. You need that solid basis. You need the people around you to be supportive, you need your family to buy in to what you are doing, to understand it and to give you some solidity and stability. I've been very lucky with that and have been able to pass the business on to wonderfully capable children, but it is not an easy task to achieve. It took a lot of planning and is one of the things in my life of which I am most proud.

Starting a business isn't like having a job. It's not just time-consuming or hard work, it is a way of life. It's not for everyone and, if you want to play the game in the higher levels, you have to be prepared for some knocks and some challenges.

But I have to say that it also brings with it huge benefits – not just financial, but in terms of satisfaction. Doing something you are passionate about, and doing it successfully, is one of the most rewarding feelings you can have. I would absolutely encourage anyone with a great idea and the drive to succeed, and the right work ethic, to go into business – but go into it with your eyes wide open.

THE EARL OF DERBY, DL

People / Different / Sustainable / Risk / Responsibility

Edward Derby's business motto is nothing short of a tongue twister - 'Prior Preparation and Planning Prevents Piss Poor Performance'. He applies this philosophy to more than 100 different charities and organisations, and as chairman of FF&P Trustee Co, a subsidiary company of the largest family office in EMEA region. His biggest business challenge, however, came from his own past. With a family line that stretches back more than 600 years and includes Prime Ministers, patrons of Shakespeare and the founder of two of the world's most famous horse races, Edward Stanley, the 19th Earl of Derby, inherited a rich heritage. But his title also came with a vast stately home in need of major refurbishments, a tired safari park, and out-dated estate buildings. His mission was to transform this inheritance into a sustainable business for the 21st century. Now, Knowsley Safari Park is an award-winning tourist attraction with more than 600,000 visitors a year, and the Hall is a leading events venue and the only stately home to offer 5* accommodation. Here he tells us about the challenges of this transformation, fulfilling his responsibilities to the community, and why it's important not to act like an ostrich and bury your head in the sand when it comes to business decisions.

I didn't grow up knowing that I would one day become Lord Derby. My father had older brothers, and it was assumed that they would have children. I certainly didn't go round from a young age with that expectation, which I think was probably a very good thing. I had an eye to the possibility, especially as time moved on, but I also had a real hunger and determination to make a success of my own life, regardless.

That hunger, that drive to do well, is something that you simply won't succeed without – especially in business. If you look at the history of Great Britain, its seafaring heritage, the Industrial Revolution, all of its innovations, they were driven by people with vision and determination. Any entrepreneur, no matter what their background, needs to have that as their bedrock.

> You may think you've come up with the best idea or product ever – and perhaps you have – but do you have the plans in place to survive until the rest of the world starts to appreciate it?

For me, inheriting the title and the estate wasn't a way into an easy life. Everything here was very tired. Safari parks were closing across the country. The costs associated with the hall were vast – a leaking roof would be a disaster financially, everything was so much bigger than in a normal building, including the costs.

But I was determined that it wouldn't be me – after more than 600 years of family history – who was the person who let the estate go downhill. I knew that there were radical changes needed to allow it to survive and thrive, that I needed to take some risks and explore different ways forward. I needed to find a way to make a stately home and its estate relevant to the 21st century.

I worked in several different financial institutions, as well as attending agricultural college, before I took over at the estate. Eventually I became Head of Private Banking at Robert Fleming & Co. All of that gave me vital experience – I know it seems obvious, but it goes without saying that if you want to run a business, you need to understand finance. You need to appreciate how the business world works, you need to know how to budget, and you need to be able to realistically plan. You may think you've come up with the best idea or product ever – and perhaps you have – but do you have the plans in place to survive until the rest of the world starts to appreciate it?

Solid planning is the way to move forward. Flying by the seat of your pants can sometimes be exhilarating, and occasionally we all find ourselves in that position, but on the whole I prefer to know my stuff, to be educated about what I am doing, and to have quite happily had all of my ideas torn apart by other people to expose their flaws before it's too late. If your idea or your plan is robust enough, it will survive that process – and people you trust looking at your business plan and saying 'well, hang on, what if this happens ...?', or 'what about that possibility?' can only help you to be better prepared. Learn from the wise old owls and mentors which life provides you with.

I also think you pick up valuable life experience from everything you do, not just from formal training or certain types of job, and for me, my time in the Army was invaluable. After Sandhurst I was commissioned into the Grenadier Guards for four years, and I genuinely don't think there is any better training ground in man management. It teaches you about psychology, and about yourself, and about thinking on your feet. You learn to stand tall, to communicate, to present yourself well.

It also teaches you a military adage that I think has stood me well in business: Prior Preparation and Planning Prevents Piss Poor Performance. A bit of a tongue twister but still as true in my business life now as it was then, when I was going out on night patrols and not wanting to get mocked by a guardsman for getting the route wrong!

Before I took over officially, I had done a lot of watching, and I knew that things at Knowsley simply weren't sustainable the way they were. There were stately homes having to sell off properties or works of art, all just to survive. I wanted something different for us, and it was going to involve a lot of challenges and taking some risks.

Prior Preparation
and Planning
Prevents Piss Poor
Performance.

Risk comes with the territory in business. It is much easier to do a salaried job and draw your wage every month if you can't deal with risk. But there is a difference between being foolish and taking educated chances, having done your homework.

Luck also comes into things we are in between Liverpool and Manchester, both big centres of commerce and population, which gave us opportunities. Other stately homes or businesses might not be in that position.

We also had the existing business of the safari park to build on, which I made my first priority. That, and renovating the cottages on the estate. Everything had to be dragged into the 20th century, and to do that I had to do what most business people have to do – get my facts sorted, come up with a plan, and go and find a friendly banker who would help us reinvest in what we had.

I thought, at the time, that the hall was at least taken care of – it was leased by Merseyside Police, which not only brought in an income, but kept that massive old building in use and stopped its decline.

However, before long, the Chief Constable told me it was no longer suitable for modern day policing, and that they would be leaving. That was a huge blow, and at first I wanted to behave like one of the ostriches in the safari park and bury my head in the sand.

But again, in business you simply cannot do that. There will be challenges. Things will go wrong. The unexpected will happen, no matter how hard you try to exert your control and plan for every eventuality. We have made mistakes all the way through, some big, some small – for example doing our research on what types of pipes we needed to fit and who should fit them, and then them leaking all over antique books and beautiful old furniture.

There will always, always be things that go wrong – but all you can do is face up to the problem, and try and find a solution. Move forward. Learn from it.

In the case of Knowsley Hall, once we found out the police were leaving, we − my then-fiancée and now wife - were initially clueless as to what to do. We looked at other options − turning it into flats, charging for entry and giving tours like Chatsworth − and basically came to the conclusion that none of those options was viable. The only choice we felt we had was to at least try and restore it to its former glory and find a use for it.

It's not been overnight − it's been the best part of 20 years in fact − and it's not what we initially planned, but it's worked, and we're incredibly proud of it. My wife has very much taken the lead on the Hall, the research and painstakingly restoring it to its former glory.

Now people can come here, hold their events, and be part of this grand, historic place, and it's made it relevant again. What felt like a huge headache has turned out to be a great success − which is often the way it works out in business, even if it doesn't feel like it at the time.

Sometimes you just need a bit of vision, and a little creativity. We had lots of out-dated buildings that were completely redundant, so in 2000 we started to convert them into offices as part of our Stanley Grange Business Village. Now we've done 50,000 square feet, and plan to double that, and there are businesses in there covering all different fields, from a micro-brewery to law firms to an obesity clinic! Again, it was about taking a negative − older buildings we had no use for − and looking at what we could do with them.

Landed estates in the past have lived off their acres, but the ones who want to be sustainable and prepared for the future need to be dynamic and entrepreneurial and embrace change. I don't think that only applies to us, but to most businesses.

It also means, of course, embracing risk. Every time there is a new phase of development, you have to go off and borrow some more millions, and each time, there is part of you wondering: will it work? Will there be a demand for this? Will we get the tenants we need and will they stay? You can be as prepared as you can, but you still need to accept that there is always a chance that things will go wrong.

Happily – touching a lot of wood – things have mainly gone right, but there is a lot of anxiety involved. Some of our businesses, like the events and the catering, have big overheads, and it's not always guaranteed that there will be big profits at the end of it.

We've learned along the way and one thing that has helped has been the fact that I am very much a cup half full kind of person. I will always try and see the positives, even in a negative. I can't actually imagine my life without challenge – I'd die of boredom if all I had to do was worry about where I was going on holiday!

I've also learned over the years to employ the very best people I can – ideally people who are better than me! Try and keep good people, but if you lose them, then don't bleat about it, go and find someone else who is just as good. Everyone has their own strengths and weaknesses, it's about finding the right team for your business.

These days, I'm involved with more than 100 different charities and organisations, ranging from the Royal Navy to the business community to the University of Liverpool, as well as being chairman of the Stonehage Fleming Trustee Company. In a way, I am fulfilling the sense of 'noblesse oblige' that the British aristocracy has always had, but I'm doing it in a way that is modern and relevant – creating jobs, supporting business, and giving back to the community.

My oldest son is set to inherit, and I always say to him: 'you don't just get the big house and the fancy name, you get all the responsibility as well.' That's the same for all business people – you have a responsibility to the staff you employ, the world you work in.

It's a role I take very seriously, whether that's through my charity work, or investing in green technologies. It's been my job to put the estate on a solid business footing, to allow it to move forward in a way that is both robust and sustainable, and fulfils our commitments. It is both a privilege and a responsibility, and one which I find extremely humbling.

PETER JOHNSON

People / Family / Risk / Change / Work

Peter Johnson was working in the family butchery
business until a chance encounter with a man selling
sausage skins changed everything. That change led him
to become the now former owner of two football clubs
and a founder of Park Group plc – a business which
started with Christmas hampers and is now the UK's
leading multi-redemption voucher and prepaid gift
card business, with a turnover of £400m and 1,000
employees. Recently retired, here Peter tells us about the
importance of luck, knowing when to cut your losses,
treating people fairly and why he never imagined failure.

My father was a butcher, and owned a small chain of shops in the area. So, after achieving what we should probably call mixed results at school, that's where I started my career. I left school one Friday, and by 6am the next morning I was at work – that's the environment I was raised in, and I think it played a key part in how I developed.

> Anybody who thinks they are going to come up with a great idea, and the world will fall at their feet, is very much mistaken.

My whole family was very entrepreneurial, going back to my great-grandfather. Everybody worked very hard, and that work ethic is absolutely invaluable. Anybody who thinks they are going to come up with a great idea, and the world will fall at their feet, is very much mistaken. Above all else, business is about hard work; putting the hours in, making the effort. It can be an absolute slog, and you can't shy away from that.

For me, that started very young, working in the shops at the weekend. Then I became apprenticed, to learn the butchery trade properly – you don't want to come near me when I have a knife, believe me! It's a very hard industry, getting up at the crack of dawn to take deliveries and open shops. It's very demanding – but you get nowhere without the willingness to work.

My stroke of luck came with a man called Ray, who regularly used to come in to the shop and try and sell me sausage skins which I never bought because they were too expensive. I liked him, though, and we'd always have a chat. During the course of a cuppa, he asked me if I'd ever considered doing Christmas hampers, where people paid a small sum each week so they could have everything they needed at Christmas.

Essentially, it was a savings scheme and, although the business is very different now than it was then, that remains the same concept. This was back in the 60s and I thought it was a very good idea, so I got cards and posters printed up, and in the first year we sold 600. I was delighted. Each year, that went up and up – to the point where, when my father retired and asked if I wanted to take over the butchery business, I said no, I wanted to pursue the hampers instead.

Partly, it was a sense of independence, and wanting to do my own thing. Partly, I had simply had enough of a very tough way of life. But I could also see that the world was changing, that businesses like ours would become less important. In business, having an awareness of change is vital – you always need to pay attention to what is going on around you, and see both the potential opportunities and potential risks.

You need to think creatively, and have vision – ideally you combine that with some proper business analysis, but in my case I have to say I always operated more on instinct than anything else!

As the business grew, that's what I did. We expanded across the country, region by region, until we were national. Then logistical problems partly inspired the next phase: how do you get a turkey to Colchester without it defrosting? The answer was vouchers. People could save for vouchers which they could spend anywhere – it began with Dewhurst, then Woolworths, and now of course so many different retailers. Again, it was about seeing a potential problem and thinking about how you could both address it, and grow a new idea from it.

You have to be willing to keep moving, to adapt and to work hard. Sometimes I look back now and think 'how did I do all of that'? – but at the time, I simply never imagined failure. I had a real drive, real ambition. That, I genuinely believe, isn't something you can learn – it's something you either have or you don't. That's not to say that you can't learn many other things as you progress, but that initial determination is often simply inside you. I wanted to succeed – and I knew I could. I was confident, I had belief – I couldn't foresee a scenario where it didn't work. What I was doing made perfect sense to me.

That's not to say that everything was plain sailing. Of course it wasn't. But my core business – the hampers, the vouchers – has always gone well. It's been the peripherals that have sometimes not succeeded so well, the side projects.

My advice to people when they are in that position is to know when to close something down. It's easier said than done when you've invested time and money and energy into a project, and that's why we often let failures drag on for longer than we should. Sometimes you simply have to accept that it's not working, and rip the plaster off. Learn from your mistakes, and move on.

> Sometimes you simply have to accept that it's not working, and rip the plaster off.

When you first start out in business, it can be a very lonely existence. You are working every hour God sends, you have this vision of what you want to achieve, but you are often completely alone. At the start it was me, a girl and a dog. As you become more successful, the key is to surround yourself with people who can help – I couldn't have taken the business this far all by myself.

Don't be worried about taking on people who are brighter than you, or better at certain things than you are – the main thing is that they also need to be people who you trust, people who are loyal. If you treat your staff fairly, always, then they will treat you fairly. Your people are the single most important element of your business. We have a very low staff turnover, and people want to work here – and that stems from treating people with fairness and respect, building an environment they want to be part of.

Looking back, I can see that I was always searching for the next challenge, even if I didn't recognise it at the time. Moving from hampers to vouchers, buying Tranmere and Everton, getting involved with floating a freight company. There was never a time I sat back and thought 'well, that's my job done'. The skills and attributes which help you succeed in one aspect of business can

Just do it. Don't think about it instead, or plan it but never take the risk – do it.

be transferred to others – I liked being able to look at the next project, even if it was a football club, and think about how I could apply those skills.

Obviously, as you move through life, some of your attitudes change and evolve, they have to. I started a charitable organisation, the Johnson Foundation, in the 1980s. I felt – still feel – that it's important to try and put something back, not just through charity, but through the way you treat the people who work for you.

Being the boss brings a lot of responsibility. You are responsible for people's livelihoods – to some extent, you hold their future in your hands. That's important to remember, to not lose sight of.

There's also a legacy to be left. I may have retired, but it's important to me to see the company continue to grow and develop, to continue to thrive. I like to think I've put a solid team in place, and there is no reason why the group won't carry on doing as well as it currently is.

Your priorities will change as you go through life. To start off with, when it's just you and your idea and your hard work, the rest of life has to fit in around it. These days, I take a great deal of pleasure from being with my family. I'm lucky that I can look back and think, 'well, I might have done a few things differently' but, ultimately, I'm very happy with my lot.

Starting out in business is daunting, and it's hard at the very beginning to imagine yourself in those later stages, where you can look back on it all and have some thinking space.

The main thing I would say to anybody who is in that position, starting out for themselves, is to simply do it. Just do it. Don't think about it instead, or plan it but never take the risk – do it. I found myself at a crossroads when I could have continued with a solid family business, and instead took a gamble on the hampers. I believed in myself, and I did it. If you spend too much time questioning yourself, nothing will happen – you might not fail, but you definitely won't succeed.

Remember, all the way through, that you need to work hard. Work like you've never worked before. Trust your instincts. Keep your focus and don't get distracted. Run your luck, and make the most of opportunities and ideas. And always – right from the very start – treat people fairly.

PROF. KEVIN MORLEY

People / Different / Succeed / Money / Motivation

What happens when all of your high-achieving brothers go to Oxford University, and you drop out of Surrey to sell fish tanks instead? According to Kevin Morley, you develop your 'niggle' – the thorn under your skin that gives you the drive to succeed in life. Now, after a career that has involved turning around the fortunes of the Rover Group, launching a marketing company that grew to be the sixth biggest agency in the world, becoming an Honorary Professor of Business, starring in Secret Millionaire and almost buying Rolls Royce company, Kevin is still driven to be better, to be passionate, and to keep his brain busy. Here he tells us about the power of enthusiasm, the need for hard work, and why money alone should never be your motivation. He also describes one of his failed investments – in a little business that later became known as Uber...

I was not what you would call a good student. My mother used to lock me in the lounge to try and keep me in and get me to work, but my friends would break me out and I'd escape through the window and go to the pub instead!

All three of my brothers went to Oxford and were very high-flying academically. I, however, went to Surrey, where again I spent a lot of my time drinking. I knew where the bar was but had no idea how to find the library, and dropped out after a year and half to sell fish tanks instead.

> If you're good, your boss will notice and you'll be promoted. If he doesn't notice, move on to a better boss.

It was only when I was older that I started to realise the value of an education, and went on to gain an MSc and an MBA. Things have obviously worked out for me, but I do still regret not making the most of my education at the right time, and would urge students to take it seriously. It might not be like the real world, especially when it comes to business, but it is very valuable. It says something about you.

So, after the fish tanks, I got headhunted to a different firm, then another, and eventually ended up joining Ford. I was promoted 11 times in the nine years I was there, and I think a lot of that is down to attitude. I was the person who was energetic and enthusiastic, who had a lot of self-confidence, who loved what I was doing. People respond to that – both above and below. If you're good, your boss will notice and you'll be promoted. If he doesn't notice, move on to a better boss.

Even if you are working for somebody else's organisation, to succeed at senior levels you need to think like an entrepreneur, not an employee. Success does not come to people who work 9-to-5 and clock off on time. I was working ridiculous hours quite early on in my career – I'd be there at 6am, and often not leave until 2am. On nights I left 'early', I would join colleagues in the pub at 10 and they'd already been there for hours.

All of this, obviously, comes at a price. As my wife reminds me occasionally, I basically never saw our children until they were five or six. It's not easy – but if you want to succeed, you can't become distracted. It's very hard to combine that level of ambition and work ethic with a family life, or with anything else that takes your focus away from the job.

If you want balance, and you want weekends away with the family, then fine – but change your expectations accordingly. You simply can't afford to relax – not ever, but especially at the beginning. It can all disappear so quickly.

I've also seen people lose motivation once they have money. If we've bought a company, and the boss suddenly has £2m in his pocket, sometimes he will lose interest. If money is what drives you, what inspires you, then long-term you won't be truly successful because you might simply have enough. Money is a way of keeping score, and don't get me wrong, I like spending it but, for me, it's not what interests me.

Like many successful people, I have that niggle. The thorn under my skin that drives me on. That sense that I need to achieve – in my case, because my brothers were so much more studious than me. If the only motivation was money, I would have stopped long ago.

For me, it's about constantly wanting to improve. To succeed. To move forward. Working in business has allowed me to meet so many interesting people, to work in so many different and interesting sectors. I need that – I need fresh challenges, I need to be fascinated, I need to be learning new things all the time. I need to wake up and think, 'well, today is going to be bloody brilliant!'.

Now, obviously, I'm a human being, and I don't always feel that. There will be days full of delightful things like tax audits, or awful meetings, or days that feel a bit doomed. In business, you can face an element of adversity every single day – just deal with it. You can't afford to let those things, either the everyday problems or the big setbacks, knock you off course, of affect your self-belief.

Success does not
come to people
who work 9-to-5
and clock off on
time.

I've faced my share of issues. When I was running my marketing agency, a new person took over at Rover, which was our biggest client, and I knew our days were numbered. So I sold the company and moved on. It sounds cold, but I would advise people not to get too attached to their business, or to their product – because there may be a time when you need to move, or to sell it. Don't fall in love with something you might not have forever.

There was another time when I invested £50,000 in a project to do with taxis – a piece of software that allowed people to book, pay for and log taxis. Sounded like a great idea but at the time, 2005, it was a complete fail. It later went on to be Uber, and is now worth billions – but not to me!

We all get knocks. Learn from your mistakes. Don't stay down. Don't get distracted, either by success of by failure – keep your focus. You can't plan for everything. You can do your homework, you can work hard, but none of us can control everything that happens, can we? Nobody can control when a world event like 9/11 will happen, that changes everything. We take risk every time we walk out of the front door, or drive our car. Life is all about the unexpected – you just need to cope with it. You can't let it paralyse you or make you miserable.

When I left Rover to set up my own business, I went from having a secretary and a chauffeur and being at the top of a huge organisation to making my own coffee, on my own in an office in London. That was risk – but it was something I'd wanted to do for so long. It was exciting. It was challenging. It ignited something in me, and I wanted more.

One thing I learned earlier in my career was about finding the right people to work with. I was at Ford and basically started to realise that, to get the promotions I wanted, I had to ensure there were good people to replace me. I had to recruit potential stars, cherry pick the best. Surrounding yourself with brilliant people who are better than you is invaluable. People are more important than numbers. Knowing how to motivate people is not an optional skill, it's 100% vital.

Part of that is probably instinctive, part is learned. For example, I tend to motivate through enthusiasm. Attitude starts at the top. If you're determined, your people will be determined. If you have energy, they'll have energy. When I started at Rover, people were so demoralised you'd hear them saying they'd prefer to be on the dole, and they actually seemed ashamed to be driving our cars.

> Anybody who is not nervous about stepping into a room and talking in front of thousands of people needs their head examining.

You're not going to change people's minds by moaning, are you? They need to see you lead by example, they need to see your enthusiasm so they can respond to it. They need to believe you when you stand in front of them saying 'hey, this is going to be great – join me!' In that situation, we needed to pick people up and throw them around a bit. A lot of that is done through sheer force of will, sweeping others along with you.

I am a naturally enthusiastic and energetic person but equally so, I'm sure that my brain has figured out that my enthusiasm and energy has worked, that it's done the job, so I've also learned to use it.

That said, I am still always nervous when I have to give a speech, face people, talk in public. I was once waiting to give a speech and had an internal debate about how much I'd be willing to pay someone to do it for me. I think I ended up at about £250,000!

It's natural – a lot of the most successful people I have met can come across as tremendously confident, but also have a layer of insecurity. Those who think they are completely brilliant rarely are and you can meet a hugely effective and rich business person who is worried that, eventually, the bubble will burst and everyone will see through them.

It's natural to have occasional doubts or nerves. It shows you're a human and not a psychopath – anybody who is not nervous about stepping into a room and talking in front of thousands of people needs their head examining. The key is to use that as an extra level of motivation, to fake it till you make it as they say, and never, ever let it control you.

I've heard it said that barristers are actors in wigs, and business people are actors in suits – you can't go into a big meeting and say 'I had a bit of a skinful last night, I'm not feeling too good', or complain. You are there to inspire!

You need to appear confident, even if you don't always feel it. You need to make decisions with confidence – but don't be surprised if later, in private, you find yourself questioning them.

Questioning yourself is another way you learn, and continuing to learn is essential – staying busy, staying interested. For me, that means keeping a few plates spinning at once. Not too many, not too few, which in my case seems to be around five or six different roles or concerns.

I'd recommend that anyone in business considers taking up some non-exec positions, and builds some involvement in a world outside your own. Avoid tunnel vision where the only business that matters is yours, the only sector that exists is the one you operate in. Working with different people in different industries keeps you fresh, healthy, on your toes.

Just make sure you don't spin too many plates, and let one fall. I almost did that recently. I have a 5-star hotel in Barbados and that was a plate that almost crashed to the ground. I didn't go out there, didn't show any interest and, before I knew it, both the manager's golf handicap and bookings were at an all-time low.

I managed to catch that plate before it hit the ground and now we are having a record year – but that was my fault. I lost interest, or at least I didn't show interest – and if the man at the top isn't showing interest, how can you expect everyone else to?

SIR TERRY LEAHY

People / Change / Believe / Risk / Problems

Lifetime Achievement Award (Director magazine), Business Person of the Year (Sunday Times), European Businessman of the Year (Fortune), and a knighthood for services to food retailing – Sir Terry Leahy's is an unlikely story of the son of Irish immigrants raised on a council estate in Liverpool, proving that no circumstances can be an obstacle to one's determination. Having started as a shelf stacker at Tesco in his teenage years, little did he know that by 1997, he would become the company's chief executive, helping to transform it into one of the biggest and most influential retailers in the world. Now, as an investor in entrepreneurial businesses among his other successful ventures and interests, Sir Terry shares his views on what he believes creates the foundation for success.

I think one of the basic principles of success is that you need to be prepared to work very, very hard for it. Whether you are running your own business or whether you are joining a big existing organisation and trying to work your way up, you will need to put in the effort. We all need a little luck in life – but without the work, you won't get anywhere. Success isn't usually instant, it's based on hard work, which people can sometimes forget.

> Success isn't usually instant, it's based on hard work, which people can sometimes forget.

Secondly, I think you need to be optimistic. You need to believe that positive change is possible – that you can change things for the better, either in your own life or your business or the company you work for. If you don't genuinely believe that, if you are negative about the potential for improvement, you won't really get anywhere. You have to think you can make a difference, that your ideas and your hard work can make a difference.

It's also about how to look at what you are doing and see the ways you can make a difference. You need to find a channel for your efforts, to decide what can be made better, and what can be improved. There are plenty of people out there who never find that channel, and their efforts are wasted.

One of the things I always tried to do at Tesco was to look at the whole organisation – not just my job, or my department, but the business in its entirety. I looked at what Tesco as a business was trying to achieve, and taking that kind of overview allows you to think creatively, to have ideas, to find ways to improve things and achieve goals. It also gives you the confidence to know when something is worth taking a risk for.

Some people seem to be naturally more adept at certain things than others, including taking risk – having an instinctive grasp of evaluating risk, or the timing of when to take those risks. Others develop those kinds of judgements as they go on, with experience, but either way, it is an important part of business life.

So is being challenged, or finding yourself in difficult positions. We've all faced problems and no matter how successful people appear to be, they will have faced difficult issues and times when things went badly wrong. But every time you face adversity, every time something goes wrong, you can get through it and learn from it.

I've learned over the years that when things do go wrong, persistence is one of the most important attributes to have. You need to have faith and determination. You can't simply give up if things get too difficult, or if they don't go right first time. You have to carry on working at it, you have to keep going, and you have to keep your belief that eventually you will overcome the problems you are facing. That's where the optimism comes in – staying hopeful gives you a lot of motivation to stick at things.

> I think one of the problems in society is that we are all terrible judges of ourselves.

By that I don't mean you should carry on doing what you're doing even if it's wrong. If something isn't working, it's important not to keep repeating the same mistakes and hoping for a different outcome. Carrying on unchanged won't work – you need to look at the situation, figure out what is going wrong, and try to fix it.

In my experience, from what I've seen in business over the years, people can be held back by a fear of failure. A lot of the time, that is misplaced fear – a fear of making their boss unhappy, of getting told off, of losing their job.

In a big organisation, you see that happening with people. This kind of fear means that they never really commit to what they are doing, they never really fulfil their potential or really make their mark in the way they could. In a big organisation, someone like that can avoid taking risks, and spend their days pushing paper and avoiding situations that make them fearful. But avoiding the risks also means not being the best they can.

I think one of the problems in society is that we are all terrible judges of ourselves. None of us really knows what qualities we have, especially in terms of these kinds of business-related skills. There isn't an objective yardstick to judge it by. I'd say people should be careful not to judge themselves too harshly – if you do that, you'll put a limit on yourself, and possibly never know what it is you're actually capable of.

It's also important to remember that wherever you come in at on the spectrum of natural abilities, there are ways to make it better. That's another thing you have to remain optimistic about – your own ability to change and learn.

If I didn't genuinely believe in that, I wouldn't have had the career I've had. If you grow up like I did, on a council estate, there are certain paths you are expected to take. I passed the 11-plus exam and had a scholarship to St Edward's College, which was a very good fee-paying school with an excellent reputation.

I was lucky, and it gave me a potential path to a different kind of life. After school, I went to university, which gave me the qualifications I needed to move on. Having access to that opportunity, to the chance to change my future through a good education, was of absolutely massive value to me. It literally changed everything.

There are certain institutions that will provide young people with those opportunities, with the support and the encouragement they need – maybe a church, or a great school. It makes an amazing difference to people's lives and is not to be underestimated.

As you go through life, it is inevitable that you will be influenced by the experiences you have, by your childhood, by the people around you. It's impossible not to be – and sometimes it influences you negatively, and sometimes positively. But you can usually learn something from it.

We all need a
little help along
the way.

I mentioned luck earlier on, and everybody could do with a little luck. It's not always obvious, it can come in different forms, like being around certain people. Sometimes other people see things in you that you don't necessarily see yourself – that can be in the workplace, or at school. We all need people who believe in us, we all need a little help along the way.

I was lucky enough to have people who helped me during my earlier days, both at school and at work. People who were a tremendous support to me. Giving somebody a helping hand, some encouragement or some advice, can have very profound effects on their lives. I've been on the receiving end of it, and I hope I've always tried to pass that on as well. At Tesco, I was always keen to spot new talent, to encourage them, and I still do that now in different ways.

Looking back over my career, and the journey that I've been on and that we all go on in different ways, I can see times when I had to adjust the way I looked at life and at work.

One of the big transitions you go through is learning to work through other people. Earlier on in life, much of what you do centres entirely around your own needs and your own goals. At school, if you are starting your own business, or in a workplace, to begin with you focus on what you are doing, what your ambitions are, and how you are going to succeed. That is what matters the most: yourself.

But gradually, as you progress through life and your career expands, you realise that changes. Eventually, it becomes just as important that you not only motivate yourself, but that you motivate other people. You need to inspire the people you work with, and motivate them to get the results you want them to get. It's a big change in attitude, and an important one in leadership. You can't do everything yourself, you have to lead other people to do it with you. Even though I have retired from Tesco, I am still working – just not in quite the same way. When people ask me what I'm up to these days, I say I am busy getting on with enjoying life!

In all seriousness, I think the most that anyone can ask for is to lead a life that is full and useful, and where you are trying to achieve something worthwhile. And if you can make a few bob from it as well, even better!

IAN AYRE

People / Learn / Opportunities / Mistakes/ Communication

Liverpool Football Club is a global brand known and respected around the world. With a revenue of more than £255m, its own TV channel, 30m social media followers and a place in the top ten of the Deloitte Football Money League, it's not just about sport – it's about business. CEO Ian Ayre has nursed the club he supported as a child back to financial health, championed its expansion plans, and brokered some of its biggest deals. As he spends his last year with his beloved LFC, he talks to us about the need to be 100% challenged, the importance of staying calm, and how a stint in the Navy prepared him for the business world.

I grew up in the shadow of Anfield, and pretty much everyone in my immediate family supports Liverpool. I'm proud to work for the club and to be from the city, but leaving school at the time I did, in 1979, there weren't many options.

Liverpool wasn't the place it is now. Socially, economically, politically, there were a lot of problems and not that many opportunities. I could have been a bit of a scallywag, truth be told, and I knew I needed a job that would challenge me and keep my brain engaged. None of the choices I was looking at by staying at home fitted that description, so I decided to join the Navy.

I was only 15 when I signed up, and 16 when I joined. I worked in the military for ten years, working at times with the Navy, the Marines, and the Air Force. I ended up in Hong Kong working in communications, which is what bridged the gap between the teenaged me leaving school and the me who ended up working in business.

I'd developed a real feel for Asia, for its culture and nuances, and I joined Pace Micro Technology, which made set-top boxes for satellite TV. That was the beginning of my work as a business person, but being in the military had taught me some valuable lessons – ones I still use today, and that I think are useful in all walks of life.

Apart from anything else, it helped me grow up. Even now, I sometimes meet people and I know if they have a military background; there is a certain maturity there that doesn't come from other life experiences.

I learned to get on with people, to put my personal feelings aside, and to recognise other people's strengths and weaknesses. If you're stuck in a camp, or on a ship, with 20 other men, you can't just have a tantrum or decide to move if someone annoys you. So you develop tolerance.

I think leaders need that – they need to be able to accept other people for what they are, and work with them for the best results.

Perhaps it goes without saying that it also teaches you discipline – but real discipline, not like being told off by your mum and dad! If you mess up in the military people can die. While I was serving, there were conflicts such as the Falklands, Northern Ireland, the first Gulf War – serious stuff, that makes you appreciate later in life what a real problem is.

> If you're the one screaming and panicking in the middle of a crisis, how is everyone else supposed to react?

I mean, in business you will face challenges and tough situations and problems that you have to work really hard to overcome. But ultimately, a deal that goes wrong or a manufacturing issue, or someone losing a football match, is not a matter of life and death is it? There is a big difference between a problem with a player or a profit margin and global strife.

That's something I've always carried with me and which has given me the strength to deal with tricky situations. The worst that could probably happen is losing my job and I knew I'd always get another one.

It's also given me the ability to stay calm, even in the middle of a storm. That matters, because people look to their leaders to do that – to guide them and reassure them. If you're the one screaming and panicking in the middle of a crisis, how is everyone else supposed to react? Leaders can't afford to get caught up dramas that aren't really dramas.

The way you lead, the way you manage, will trickle down throughout your organisation, so you have to ask yourself what kind of a place do you want to be running? People will look to you to set the tone, so it's essential that you try and get it right. That's about the way you act yourself, and the standards you display in your own behaviour, but also about the team you assemble.

That's been one of the big challenges at Liverpool, pulling together a great team on and off the pitch. I'm not interested in big and loud and verbose – those sorts of people rarely achieve anything that matters. I'm interested in professionals who work hard, who are passionate but also respectful. People who can work as individuals, and bring their own skills and attributes, but who can also work as part of a team culture.

Anybody running their own business, or working in business, needs to be aware of that, and of the impact of the management and leadership style they introduce. The wrong people at the top can lead to real problems lower down, and then the whole organisation suffers.

Personally, I think it's also essential that people who work with you feel they have the opportunity to rise through the ranks, that their hard work will be rewarded. You need to create opportunities for good people and if those opportunities aren't there at that time, be honest about it and allow them to move on.

Ambitious people are always looking for opportunities, and that includes me. One of my defining characteristics has always been the need to be challenged, and to find opportunities that will allow me to wake up every day feeling driven and motivated. Once that challenge starts to fade, I know it's time to move on – I've often been called crazy for leaving what seem to be very comfortable situations purely to look for the next challenge!

I was the CEO at Pace in Asia after an IPO, and people thought I had it made, but that's when I knew it was time to find something else, something that would make me feel energised. It's one of the reasons I'm leaving Liverpool next year – I still love the job, and I'm very proud of lots of our achievements here, but I've done a lot of what I set out to do and the time is right to go and give someone else the chance!

I know many people will see that as a crazy choice, and I know the Red half of the city will especially think I'm mad, but I need to be chasing a goal.

I don't think that attitude – that drive – is something you can learn. I think that's something you are born with, that's in your DNA, and maybe it's honed by your family life or your environment in your early years.

I think coming from certain places shapes you. Certainly, Liverpool people, myself included, are not short of an opinion or the confidence to speak out. I've learned, over the course of my career, that sometimes that kind of honesty really pays off – just telling it like it is. When I was in the Navy, I once told an Admiral that all the messages I had for him were a load of rubbish and not worth reading. He was shocked, but he'd asked and I answered honestly! On that occasion it worked, and it forged a bond between us based on honesty.

On other occasions, it doesn't work. I had one boss who was a complete tyrant, and I had to go and face him after I'd made a bit of a mess up with some accounts. I got there and he was sweating and fuming and so angry. I started the conversation with the line 'so, you're pretty upset then?' – which I'd hoped might deflate the tension, but actually just made it all worse!

> Anyone who thinks they have nothing left to learn has failed.

At the very least, though, I think being on the outspoken side does get you noticed. Being honest, being passionate, makes you stand out – it makes sure you don't become the grey man who nobody ever remembers.

So as you go through life, I think you learn to blend those natural skills and characteristics with experience. You develop instincts and you continue to learn. I learn every single day – and I hope I never stop. You can learn from the good and the bad, from the people you want to be like, and the people you don't want to be like. You should soak it all up like a sponge.

Anyone who thinks they have nothing left to learn has failed – people who think they've 'made it', and can now sit back and be pompous and think they're always right, are going nowhere.

I hope I'm always big enough to recognise that there is always something I can learn, to recognise my own strengths and weaknesses, and to be prepared to always listen. Having your own core values and sticking to them is important, but so is listening to other people and being able to accept your own imperfections.

Everything you learn in life, from being a child onwards, gets stored away in your mind. No experience is wasted – you often find that something you learned years before ends up getting re-used in a completely different scenario.

Lessons I learned early on included the power of good communication, and taking responsibility for your mistakes.

When I was with Pace, we had a manufacturing problem with some products we provided to Star TV in India. I had to fly from our office in Hong Kong to Mumbai to deal with it, and go to a meeting with senior members of their board. I had to simply take a beating, which didn't come easily as I was still quite young, and had to acknowledge what had gone wrong – as well as assuring them the problem would be dealt with. Apologising for your mistakes is the first step towards fixing them.

Funnily enough, I met the client at a conference years later and they actually remembered that meeting! Everyone makes mistakes and sometimes they feel like the end of the world. You need to remember that it's not the end of the world, and that mistakes are fine as long as you learn from them.

Communication is one of the most important tools you will use in business. Be honest. Tell people what you are planning and trying to achieve. That way, by keeping the lines of communication open, you can avoid surprises, and try to see around corners.

Running a football club isn't quite like running any other business. You can plan for things, but you can't guarantee they will happen. Say, for example, you're talking about the Cup Final – you have to plan for winning it, and losing it, and something going wrong. It's impossible to accurately budget as you can't accurately forecast what is going to happen – the Champions' League, for example, could add £40-£50m to our income, but you can't count on it.

You can have meetings and plan and do all the stuff a normal CEO does, but at the end of the day it depends on 11 blokes kicking a ball around a pitch at the weekend! Everyone has an opinion on what you're doing and how you're doing it, and you invite 46,000 opinions into your house every home match – it's different, and good communication is absolutely vital.

You need to be able to communicate with everyone in business, not just the ones you think might matter. For me, I need to be able to communicate with other business people, with partners, sponsors, staff, players, the manager, the fans.

Being a leader means you don't have the luxury of just chasing the prize. It's not just about money or a short term goal. I've seen people fail because of that – they are so focused just on making money, that there is no proper strategy, no underlying infrastructure that makes what they are doing sustainable.

I think some of the achievements I'm most proud of at Liverpool are the ones that support that kind of long-term goal. Our new stand, the way it has become a reality, is a legacy I'm proud of – for the club, and for the city.

I've enjoyed every minute of working here, but I'm also looking forward to what comes next and I'm open to suggestions as to what that is!

Life is short, and I need to wake up every morning and feel like I won't waste a second of any day.

ASIF HAMID

People / Attitude / Plan / Success / Understand

In his early 20s, Asif Hamid – like many other people of his generation – got a job in a call centre. But, unlike most of those other people, Asif went on to rise not only within that organisation, but in business, eventually launching The Contact Company with just 15 staff. Since then, he has gone on to become an award-winning entrepreneur running an ever-expanding £20m+ organisation, employing more than 1300 in his growing team and building two brand new call centres from scratch. With a client list which includes the likes of River Island, Superdrug and Argos, Asif has ambitious plans to expand ever further. Here he tells us why he thinks entrepreneurs stand out in a crowd, and why chasing success is more important than chasing the cash to buy a nice car.

I started working in a call centre as an agent, as something of a stop-gap to be honest. I wasn't really sure what I wanted to do with my career or my life. I knew I wanted to succeed, but I wasn't convinced at what. So I took the job there, and it's fair to say it changed everything. In a way, that was a stroke of luck, coming across a path I knew I could follow, by chance. But luck only goes so far. It presents you with an opportunity. It's up to you how you take it from there.

> Luck only goes so far. It presents you with an opportunity. It's up to you how you take it from there.

For me, I realised that the customer contact industry was one I could really thrive in. Apart from anything else, I loved it – it was fun! I enjoy being around people, talking to people, learning from people. I've never lost that. In those early days, I had a great boss – he was a very flamboyant, inspiring individual. He worked hard and had a real flair for what he was doing, plus he drove a very nice car!

I knew I wanted to drive a nice car to, and perhaps, when we start out, those kinds of things are good motivating factors. I saw what he had achieved, and became convinced that this was the right world for me. That I could make a mark here. So I worked hard and I was good at what I did, and I rose through the company. Eventually I was headhunted to another business – which was great experience, but what I really wanted to do was start my own. In 2006, The Contact Company was born – with just 15 staff.

Obviously we've come a long way since then. We now have around 1300 staff, and plan to have a £40m turnover within the next five years. And, ironically, when I started out I was an agent handling calls for Argos which is now one of our clients, so that's come full circle!

I think I was successful for a few different reasons. I think entrepreneurs stand out – in a crowd and in a workplace. There's a certain work ethic, a positive attitude, a self-belief. A real commitment to making things work. If my boss came to me and asked if I could do something, I'd do my very best to make it happen, no matter how tough it was. I'm not saying I could achieve the impossible – but the management knew that if it was possible, I'd do it. That makes you stand out for all the right reasons.

I grew up in a two-up, two-down terraced house, in a single parent family. I didn't come from anything fancy – but one thing my mother always taught me, from a very early age, was the importance of respecting other people. If you combine that respect with hard work, with determination, with creative thinking, and with good communication, you're off to a head start.

People have been at the heart of everything I've done in my career. I've always been good at building networks, developing relationships, at communicating. That's absolutely vital – not just talking, but listening. When I was working for other people, I would listen, and look, and learn. I'd take everything I could from what they were doing and then I'd start thinking about how it could be done better. I think that's a key attribute that an entrepreneur has – always looking for ways to improve, to be better.

When the time comes for you to make that leap, to start your own business perhaps, or to make the next move within your career, you have to be prepared. You have to know your stuff, inside out, whatever your sector is. You can't lead if you don't know what you're doing. Decide your goals, but make sure you have them as short, medium and long term.

There's no point running before you can walk – if you shoot for the stars from day one, you may feel like a failure if you don't achieve that straight away. In reality, that happens to very few people – you might look at a successful businessman and think he has it all, that it looks easy, but I can guarantee that it hasn't been easy!

That businessman or woman will have worked very hard; a lot of effort will have gone into making their success look effortless. For us, we started small – just some great ideas about the industry, about quality and service, and only 15 staff.

Pretending you get
something when
you actually don't
will always have
consequences in
the end.

I was already doing well in my job and starting my own business was a risk. Like all risks, it was about weighing up the tangible stuff – analysing the data, looking at the positives and negatives – but also knowing when to trust your instincts. Ultimately that risk paid off for me and my team, but that doesn't mean that everything has been easy. There have been some very difficult times.

We started in 2006, just before the recession kicked in. One of our major clients was Woolworths, and they went under in 2007. At the time, that was a huge blow. The recession also meant a real change in attitude from the banks, so you couldn't assume they would play ball any more. It was a huge challenge – but we got through it because we'd planned for it. It was time to roll up our sleeves, work hard, and tough it out.

There's an old saying, hope for the best but plan for the worst, and I always plan for the worst. Cash is king and you need to always plan for when things go wrong.

On a more personal level, I had a very low point when a senior member of staff crumbled under the pressure of the job, and eventually left. I felt like I'd failed that person, that I could have supported them better, helped them to get through it and fulfil their potential. That hit me hard – mentoring people is very important to me. But all I could do was look at it, figure out what I could have done differently, and move on, stronger in the knowledge that I'd learned from what was a very difficult situation.

The flipside of that kind of professional and emotional investment in people is the satisfaction you feel when they thrive. We have a mentoring scheme and there are staff in it from all different roles and walks of life, but they all have something in common – potential. With them, as it was with me when I was starting out, there is a certain spark that makes them stand out. I can see it more clearly now it's not about me – it's a certain attitude.

Attitude is a hard thing to manufacture. You can teach other things. You can teach processes, and technology and techniques. But attitude is personal, it's all your own. I like being around people who are like leeches, in the nicest possible way. They soak up all the information and experience around them and use it to their own advantage. They're disciplined and they're passionate. You can see the possibilities in them – and if you're just starting out, it's up to you to show those attributes.

I've learned a lot over the years, obviously. One thing I knew from the very beginning was that surrounding myself with a top-class team would be vital. Never be afraid to employ people who are better than you, or more successful than you. I've had the same team since I started out and it makes all the difference.

I've learned a lot about managing people. Shouting is never the best way to get what you want, and being honest and respectful is the key. Again, that's something I was taught in my childhood and you see people who skipped that lesson suffer at some point down the line. No matter how ambitious you are, you must always remember that people come first – be honest, have integrity and lead from the front.

I live by the belief that I would never ask an employee to do something I wouldn't do myself. The people out there dealing with the calls, using the technology, doing the day-to-day job, are the ones who understand it best, and if you become distant from that, if you lock yourself up in your big office and don't mix with them, you are losing out on a massive resource. I still go and eat lunch in the staff room most days!

I'd also advise people to never be afraid to ask questions. If you're in the workplace and you genuinely don't understand something, then ask – you can never have too much knowledge. Pretending you get something when you actually don't will always have consequences in the end. Even now, I am the boss, and I am still not afraid to ask, to admit that I don't understand.

When I'm asked what I think people starting out in business need, that's one of the things I say. I'd also say they need to be resilient. There will be knocks, there will be challenges and you need to have the strength to weather the storm, both in terms of business and your personality. You need to have good people you trust and you need to have the right skills and networks. But also, and this is really important, you need to have fun with it – if you can't have fun, if you don't enjoy your work, you won't feel passionate about it. And without passion, you'll fail.

These days I am very focused on expanding the business, creating more jobs for people and supporting economic regeneration in a variety of ways. I'm thinking about my legacy as well as day-to-day business. I'm looking for sustained growth, and ways to increase opportunities for everyone who works with me. The sense of satisfaction I get at being able to do those things is enormous and definitely something that has developed over the years.

When I first started, I wanted to drive a nice car. That's about money. These days, for me, it's not about chasing money, it's about chasing success, which is different. You can get enough money for the car and lose it the next month.

Success in business is about the long-term as well. It's about quality and striving to be the best, looking at ways to improve and looking to put something back into society. There is a difference but, funnily enough, I have noticed that if you chase the success, the money often comes along with it anyway!

MAGGIE O'CARROLL

Women / Change / People / Success / Men

More than half the UK's population is made up of women – yet twice as many men as women are self-employed, and women in full-time work earn, on average, 15% less per hour than men. Striving to address inequalities such as these is Maggie O'Carroll, founder and chief executive of award-winning social enterprise the Women's Organisation, and the leading force behind the creation of the £5.3m International Centre for Women's Enterprise Development. Here Maggie, an influencer at national and international level on female economic development, shares her views on women in business, on the need for societal change, and her vision for the future.

I am originally from Ireland, but moved to the States as a student before eventually settling in Liverpool in the early 90s.

It wasn't in great shape economically at that time, and wasn't exactly bursting with opportunities. I struggled with fitting into the traditional employment model where employees were never encouraged to contribute their ideas to help improve how things were done, and there was a real sense that women were not given an equal voice despite being equally - if not better - educated and more experienced than their male counter parts. I'd been living in America where there was a very different attitude to life and to business – an attitude that anything was possible, which didn't seem to exist here.

Eventually, I turned to entrepreneurship out of necessity, although it did suit me. I've always had the ambition to row my own boat, to navigate ever-changing waters, which is definitely a skill that is very handy in business.

I initially had this idea of forming an organisation to support women; to empower them, to focus on training and development. It was very popular in the US, and I saw no reason why it wouldn't translate over here.

I was in my early 20s at the time, and went to see a business advisor about my idea. He was a grey man in a suit, very fatherly and condescending, and he basically told me I was being a bit silly and would be better off getting myself a nice little job. Looking back, it was a perfect example of exactly why it was needed!

To cut a long story short, I shelved the idea, and went into business in a different way – through publishing. So I was entrepreneur, just not in the way I'd wanted. I spent six years working in that, with trade magazines, and it was successful – but once British Rail was privatised we hit a lot of bumps as it was one of our big contractors so, essentially, I took the money and ran, did some travelling.

When I got back again, I realised that the initial idea had still not left me; that the need for it was still there – for a consultancy that would focus on women's training and development, research, working with women and with clients in the public and charitable sector. In 1996, I finally did it – I and a small group of visionary board members launched a social enterprise that was then called Train 2000, and we're now in our 20th year after rebranding as the Women's Organisation in 2010.

I've always had a clear vision, a strong sense of social purpose, and I've always been driven. I never wake up wondering what I'm doing with my life – and to do this, you need to be just as driven as if you are running a big global business. The focus is different – it's not about making millions personally, it's about driving equality and creating wealth in the regional and national economy, and recognising that 52% of the population have a part to play in that.

Like a lot of people with an initial idea, it was hard to start with. It felt like swimming against the tide. People would ask sarcastically 'where are the special men's groups'? 'Aren't you being sexist'? I'm sure some people still hold those beliefs, even if they don't always express them. The kind of stuff we had to listen to was amazing. We had meetings where even elected officials said things like 'really, there's no point in women's economic development – they're fine as they are'.

But, as ever in life, you have to get through things like that, those kinds of challenges – both direct and more subtle – and stick to your guns. Over the years, more and more men have come to see that this isn't anti-men, it's about their daughters and nieces and sisters, about a whole section of society suffering from poor pay, less promotions, a lack of opportunities. It's about the fact that a strong economy is an inclusive economy.

We've come a long way, but perhaps not at the pace I would have liked. Being patient is sometimes difficult. Despite everything that has been achieved over the last 20 years, there is still not a level playing field. Things aren't the same for Joe as Joanne. If you go to a business networking event, there simply aren't the same number of women in senior positions, or running their own business. Is that because women are less capable? Of course not – so we ask ourselves what the institutional and practical barriers are.

Sometimes it's simple, and it's about policies which have been created without a thought for half of the population and the way their lives work. Take transport as an example – a public transport system might be designed to get people to work on time, so the focus is on moving people between 7 and 9am. But what about mum, who will be doing the school run then, and then needs to get to work later? It's about looking at things from these angles – gender-proofing everything.

> It's all about giving yourself the best chance to be heard.

Over the years, the role of the Women's Organisation has changed and developed. It's not only about working with women as individuals. It's about working to bring about this kind of change, which of course doesn't always make you popular. Shining a light on these issues is a big part of what I do, and that will always be a challenge. With this, as with other aspects of business, you need to know your stuff, do your homework. Understand the background before you can change the future. Feel completely passionate about what you're doing – because it's not easy, and if you don't have that passion and belief, it will be even harder.

Now, we have a very strong role to play in campaigning, advocacy, collecting data and case studies which help and influence policy makers and help the private sector recruit more effectively. Part of our job is to raise awareness – to let business owners and employers know that the best way to improve your business is through attracting the very best candidates, and to do that, you need to consider issues such as flexible working. If you don't you might be excluding more than half of the population, which isn't good for

There is a
tendency in
our society to
equate success
with money
– but it is also
about happiness,
contentment, and
social impact.

you, or your business. A woman coming back to work two days a week will give a fantastic level of productivity. Women generally have a more collaborative approach, they have tenacity, and frankly there is often less posturing and more actual doing.

I'm not saying women are better than men – that's a ridiculous statement, and one that people seemed to want to box me into in the early days – but what I'm saying is that women should have the same opportunities and access as men. That when you are recruiting or promoting, the best man or woman should be considered – even if it means looking at things a little differently.

While it's important for us to do the research, to work with academics to underpin the case for change, we also work in the real world. We understand what it is like running a business, and all the various challenges it brings. I've been lucky enough to work with some amazing business women, totally inspiring women – although they often don't want to shout about it! There are some remarkable female entrepreneurs out there, but often you'll have never heard of them because they don't like to blow their own trumpets.

But this is also important. There isn't enough profiling of successful female entrepreneurs. It's about showing other women what they can do – encouraging them and giving them the means to upskill, to climb out of economic inactivity, to get out there and look for finance, to grow ambitions that they can then share with other women. The cornerstones of the future will be built on change at a policy level, and on developing the aspirations of younger women. Role models are crucial.

From what I've seen, and from what I have learned myself personally over the years, there are a few things that women perhaps should pay more attention to. They need to invest in themselves – and see themselves as a worthwhile project. They need to focus on training and development, getting a mentor, on PR, gaining confidence around public speaking. Everyone should do this, not just women, but it is especially helpful for them when they are starting a business or looking to move upwards. It's all about giving yourself the best chance to be heard.

With age and experience, I've not lost that 'I can do it' attitude – but that's something that takes a little time to take root in people who haven't always had it. Success might be something they've not been raised to expect – also, how do they judge success? There is a tendency in our society to equate success with money – but it is also about happiness, contentment, and social impact.

For me, seeing what we've achieved so far is a mixed bag. On the one hand, we've done so much, and come so far. But on the other, there is still so much further to go – we still regularly see employers breaking the law in the way they are paying and promoting women, and there's nothing being done really to dissuade them. Until we have transparent pay, quotas, and penalties, there will be no reason for some of them to change. We can educate and convince and persuade – but ultimately, enforcing the law will help change the culture, and that is what will change society.

It's still feels like I'm pulling uphill, after all these years – but it is still something I feel, personally, I need to do. I am, in a way, just a curator working with a gifted group of stakeholders for all of these issues. I'm just the spokesperson for this agenda – the real stars are the women who are out there, living it, every single day.

GRAHAM MORRIS, OBE

People / Choice / Team / Values / Integrity

The UK car industry has seen some turbulent times: dramatic changes, constant upheaval, some losses and many wins. Graham Morris has been at the heart of those changes – and was even in the position where he made his own father redundant! Starting as a 20-something graduate at British Leyland, he worked his way up, both within that company and others, to eventually become the chief executive of Rolls Royce and Bentley, a position he quit on a point of principle. Here he tells us how his working class roots helped him; the qualities he thinks resulted in him being repeatedly promoted and how saying you have integrity, and living with integrity, are two different things.

I always wanted to work in industry, and in particular the car industry. Even though my dad couldn't drive and we never had a car, he worked for British Leyland at their plant in Speke, so it was already in the blood, so to speak.

When I got my first job – for British Leyland at Longbridge – it was in the finance department. I was promoted six times in five years until I eventually went to the Triumph plant in Speke as Financial Controller. I was 28, and the youngest financial controller the company had had.

I'd say that 98% of the people working there loved their jobs and loved the company, but there was a very disruptive minority that contributed to its problems - which was typical of all industries at that time. In the end, we had to close down one of the two factories, losing 3500 jobs. My dad, who was a senior foreman by that stage, was one of the people who was made redundant and I had to pay off. Fortunately it didn't cause any problems in the family as, deep down, my father was proud that his lad had done well, and he knew there was no alternative.

I think my roots also helped with the difficult job I had to do at that time – a lot of the staff there knew me as 'George's lad', rather than the financial controller! But obviously, it wasn't easy. It was heart-breaking when the place finally closed, knowing the impact it would have on so many families, but British Leyland was crumbling. There just wasn't any choice.

During that stressful time I received my next promotion – and this was one that came right out of the blue. I was given the job of drawing up the organisation chart for the remaining factory in Liverpool, with 2500 employees. A Group HR guy was helping and he saw something in me that I had not and suggested I become manufacturing director. I had been a finance guy for five years – and this was a real step outside my comfort zone. I think one of the attributes he saw was that I was highly inquisitive. I didn't just want to make the numbers add up, but really understand what they meant and how the business ran.

I'd be lying if I said I wasn't worried. It was a big risk and suddenly I found myself with around 2,000 people working for me, all of them being much older and more experienced managers in a completely different function. I think it helped that I was from Liverpool and I spoke their language – but it wasn't easy to start with.

In fact, I think I've felt that with every promotion. When it's been raised or discussed, part of me has secretly been thinking, hang on a minute, I'm not sure I can do that! But part of succeeding is talking yourself out of that kind of self-doubt and having the belief to take the risk – the leap of faith in yourself.

Those sorts of opportunities – the big ones that can change the direction of your career or your life – don't come around that often. You have to be realistic about it, but also you have to be optimistic. You have to see the opportunity and have the courage to go for it – prove your worth, become the person who does a good job, the person who people will then come to with other opportunities.

> Some of it is being in the right place at the right time but a lot of it is about who you are as a person.

Don't run away from the job just because you're not 100% sure you're up to the challenge. I always think the first three to six months of a new role are horrible – getting to know everyone, building relationships, finding out who you can trust. It's hard, and sometimes you feel like you've made a mistake – but eventually you will start to have more good days than bad days.

As to why certain people get these opportunities and get offered the promotions...well, that's a hard one, isn't it? Some of it is being in the right place at the right time but a lot of it is about who you are as a person. I remember with my first job, I was very young, and very respectful of authority, so I was also very quiet.

After a while, my boss took me on one side and said: 'Initially we were a bit worried about you, Graham. We can teach you all the techniques of the job, but without personality, you're never going to be able to sell your ideas to others.' Those words have stuck with me now for more than 40 years.

Now, personality doesn't have to mean being the one who is the loudest, or the cockiest, or who struts around. You don't have to be that man to get noticed. Think about the kind of person you would want on your team, or who you would want managing you. You can be lively without being arrogant; you can be intelligent and a good guy and know your stuff, have a sense of humour, behave decently, and really, really work hard to get the job done.

These qualities will get you noticed, in a positive way. You get promoted because you are good at what you do, and because you are trustworthy. Everyone knows a person who comes to work at 9am, hangs their brains up in the cloakroom, and does nothing until home time. Equally, people always notice a boss who rests on his laurels, and sneaks off to play golf every day. Successful people, I've noted – whether they are entrepreneurs or working their way up through a company – are self-driven.

They don't need to be praised to feel good about a job well done - although it is nice from time to time – they feel good already, because doing a good job is their aim. Equally, they don't need to be overly criticised when something has gone wrong because they are already hyper self-critical and probably beating themselves up about it! A self-starter is competing with himself and, because of that, they tend to have a work ethic that makes them stand out.

I can't speak for every person who ever promoted me, or say what they saw in me, but I think that is part of it. I was never someone who looked to the top and said 'that's my ambition', and desperately scrambled to get there. My ambition was always to do the very best in the job I was doing at the time – and that paid off.

I also have a very strong set of values that I think has stood me in good stead – although it hasn't always looked that way from the outside, perhaps. Certainly when I was resigning as the chief executive of Rolls Royce and Bentley, one of the most prestigious jobs in the industry, it might not have looked especially sensible. But integrity and credibility are attributes you can't just pay lip service to – they are values you have to live. And if you do live it, people will be inspired by you and they will follow you. If you don't have them – or, even worse, if you claim to be a man of principle but don't act as though you are – people will never, ever trust you.

Integrity is important. I also told my people that I would never knowingly tell them a lie. I tell people that I might not always tell them everything, but I won't outright lie. I also think it's important to remember where you came from. When I was being promoted and getting jobs that were more and more challenging and taking me further up the ladder, I always stayed true to myself. Part of that is a working class Liverpool thing – if you start being too big for your boots, there'll always be someone willing to knock you down again!

> None of us are Superman. We bleed, we cry, we suffer. We're all human.

I have seen people make that mistake – they've been promoted, and it's gone to their heads. Perhaps they've felt they needed to act differently, or that their 'real' persona wasn't good enough now. It's always a mistake. You weren't promoted for your fake personality, you were promoted because of your real one, so hang on to it, you're doing something right!

It was because of these values that I ended up leaving Rolls Royce and Bentley. The company had been bought and I was told, after assurances to the contrary, that the company would be split by VW and BMW. I'd stood in front of my staff and told them the plant in Crewe would continue to make Rolls Royce and Bentleys. For many valid reasons that decision was changed but I felt the fact that, as CEO, I was not involved in this process undermined my integrity and credibility. I was never asked if I was happy with this and, at the press conference a couple of days later, it was taken for granted that I would continue.

I sat there, feeling very angry, and went home to talk to my wife about it. I talked to some trusted mentors the next day and, eventually, I resigned. It wasn't just about the decision that had been made, it was about the way it had been made. It completely undermined my credibility and my sense of honour – how could people believe me again? Or, even if they did believe me, how could they feel secure, knowing that the important decisions were out of my hands? It wasn't easy to leave that job, but I felt like I had no choice. Interestingly enough some 12 months later I did a 30-minute interview on Radio 4 with Michael Buerk called The Choice.

Choice is an interesting thing. We all make hundreds of choices every day, from the moment we decide what time to get up, what to wear, what to eat for breakfast. Some choices are beyond our control – what sort of parents we have, where we grow up. But beyond that, we make our own. You might go to a bad school in a tough neighbourhood, but you have choice – who do you want to be? Who do you want to follow? The bully, or the defender? The loud mouth who shows off but achieves nothing, or the decent guy who works hard and listens and gets on in life? We all make these choices – and choosing the right role models, the right mentors, is a vital one.

> In business, we live and die as a team – you win as a team, and you fail as a team.

After making that choice – to leave the company - I suppose I had a bit more time to reflect. I had travelled the world, living in South Africa, the States and in Germany, and met some amazing people. I'd tried to get my work-life balance right, but there were still gaps in my four kids' lives for me, things I can only remember through looking at photos. I still loved the car industry, but I also thought it might be time to vary things, and see what I could put back into society. We weren't rich, but we were comfortable enough for me to do that.

I became an active member of six charities, and then took on some non-executive roles. I've recently finished a long contract as

Chairman of a car retail group in Moscow, which was a fascinating experience. If there's one thing I've perhaps learned in all my years of work and travel, it's that wherever you are, whatever you're doing, people are people.

The vast majority of them want to come to work, do a good job, then go home and live a nice life with their family. If you respect that, you'll get more out of them. I used to work long days, 14 hours maybe, but I'd save weekend for the family and always take my holidays – it's important and you should make sure people working for you know that it matters. No matter how many times you get promoted – or how many times you don't – none of us are Superman. We bleed, we cry, we suffer. We're all human.

It's important to remember that, and also to understand that the tone of an organisation comes from the top. In business, we live and die as a team – you win as a team, and you fail as a team. If you are the person at the top, you have that responsibility, you set that tone. Some people are shouters and screamers, and set a climate of fear. Others are different. The message you send soon spreads downwards – and if you lead with integrity, if you live those values, you'll reap your reward in the hard work your team puts in.

JAMES BARTON

Believe / People / Passion / Mistakes / Value

Like many kids of his generation, James Barton grew up
with music and nightclubs in his blood. But what makes
him different is the fact that he used that passion to found
one of the best known global clubbing brands, Cream,
launch award-winning festival Creamfields and become
known as the most influential person in the world of
electronic dance music, according to Rolling Stone
magazine. Now the president of electronic dance music
for the world's leading live entertainment company, Live
Nation, James reflects on the need for perseverance
and shares the lessons he learned from the 'chaotic
rollercoaster ride' that was his early business career.

When Cream started, I was in my early 20s and it was a huge adventure – a completely chaotic existence where we were literally making it all up as we went.

I was living in London in the week and dashing back to Liverpool at the weekends, running the club night and working in the record industry and basically never even having the chance to breathe. But that was fine – I had that energy, that drive, that belief that we could make something happen.

It probably looks, from the outside, that everything went perfectly to plan – building what started as a little weekly event into what it became, with our own record label and bar and merchandise. But the truth is there was no plan, we were completely winging it, going on instinct.

It's hard to capture just how crazy it was. With each success, we had more ambition. Every time we walked a few steps in the right direction, we'd start to run. The whole business, in those days, was based on passion and enthusiasm and what we felt was right at the time. We never had the basics in place.

We didn't have a business plan, or capital, or investors, or a finance guy. We had this tiny team, this small infrastructure, and we ran with it as fast as we could. Even when people who worked with us said 'hey, hang on...are you sure?' about something, we'd ignore them.

We said yes to everything. Yes to nights in Ibiza; yes to nights all around the world, yes to so many crazy ideas. We never stopped to assess the risk or ask ourselves if we had the capacity to do this exciting new thing. We didn't pause and wonder if we could afford it, or what the financial implications would be, or if we had the operational ability – we just said yes!

There were millions of clubs around at that time, but through a combination of luck and our own belief and creativity, we stood out. We were ready to take on the world, and weren't very good at listening if somebody said we might not quite be ready.

It's hard to look back and say I have regrets about that, because in the end it turned out just fine, but I did learn lessons from it. We should, perhaps, have sometimes said no – or at least thought things through.

To the external eye, everything looked brilliant. We were putting on these packed nights and we'd captured a really magical moment in youth culture. We were known all around the world and the brand of Cream was everywhere.

But the reality is, we had hardly any money in the bank, and our infrastructure – such as it was – was creaking under the weight of what we were trying to achieve.

With the benefit of hindsight, we really needed to pause. To take a break and look at what we were doing and the business support we needed. We were great with ideas and energy and with marketing, but the rest? We weren't even really thinking about it. There was never a strategy – essentially, when it came to the solid business foundations, there was a gaping hole. We were always trying to catch up, bolt it on as an extra as we carried on moving forward. We went from two guys good at throwing a party to two guys running a huge business, very quickly.

> You need to be punished before you get to enjoy the successes of life.

Now, as I am older and possibly wiser, I realise how risky it all was. We should have been more organised, more professional. We made mistakes that could potentially have ruined what we were doing – who knows how things might have gone if we'd had some calm, some advice, some common sense? Maybe the business side of it would have run more smoothly, or maybe we'd have simply ground to a halt once our enthusiasm was dampened. Nobody can really say.

If we'd limited ourselves, controlled our excessive plans, we might have done more – or less! You can't second guess the past – but you can learn from it.

Things will go
wrong, that is
pretty much
the only thing
you can 100%
guarantee.

Mistakes are part of the whole experience, and you need them. Cream's history shows its successes, but believe me there were plenty of misses as well as hits. There were some huge problems later on, especially around the Millennium.

I'd recently split with my business partner, Darren Hughes, who I founded Cream with, and that was basically like a very messy divorce. There was a lot of anger, and I probably wasn't thinking at my best. We decided to do these huge events across the country for the Millennium, and it was a disaster. It almost bankrupted us, after all those years of work.

But I genuinely believe that you need to be punished before you get to enjoy the successes of life. You need to suffer, to make those mistakes, to learn to cope when things go wrong – because things will go wrong, that is pretty much the only thing you can 100% guarantee.

Anybody can navigate the good times pretty easily, it's how you navigate the darker times that make you who you are. That's when you learn the true value of a person. That's the kind of experience you can use – not just in business, but in life.

For me, I see Cream in two phases. There were those early days, when I was running on fumes and had no idea what was going to happen next, and the later days. The Millennium was a wake-up call for me – we almost lost everything. After that, in some ways I grew up. I sorted things out that probably should have been sorted out much earlier.

I decided to concentrate on our core business – we'd been diluting the brand, there were Cream T-shirts and coffee mugs and MP3 players. It had all spiralled out of control; I needed to take a long look at what really mattered and think about what I wanted to build. The early years were formative and exciting, but the later years are where I made some better calls. I started to think more clearly about what we could do, what we could achieve long-term rather than next weekend.

I found an investor and got a team behind me. I filled in those gaps in my knowledge, and worked with skilful business people. We had structure for the first time, investment, a finance team, a three-year plan – the business basics, but we'd never had them before. It was about discipline, and that's what allowed Cream to adapt, to not only survive but thrive. That solid base allowed us to ride out some international storms, such as the aftermath of 9/11, and look to the future.

For the first time I felt like I'd stepped off the rollercoaster and it was a big adjustment. Then, for the first time, it was about profit and sustainable growth and adding real value to the business. By the time it was sold to Live Nation, it was in a vastly different place – and so was I.

Now I am working in the States with people in the same position I was all those years ago. I see their passion and belief, their creativity, and I also see their lack of business awareness. I've come out of the other side of that, I survived, and hopefully I can now help them as well.

> You have to survive long enough for the rest of the world to catch up!

The challenge in any creatively-driven business is finding that balance between the passion and the fact that it is actually a business. You need both aspects. In some ways, perhaps I was lucky I got the chance to ride it out – but I'm not sure it's all luck.

Luck can take you so far. We were, in those early days, in the right place at the right time with the right idea, but huge amounts of hard work went into making it happen. You need to persevere, I genuinely think that's the key.

If you have a great business idea, you will believe in it, and then your job is to persuade everybody else to believe in it. You won't get anywhere if you fall at the first hurdle or even the 100th – you have to persevere, learn, pick yourself up and carry on.

There's no magic formula here – you just can't give up. Believe in what you are doing, and keep at it. For a while, you might be the only one believing. You have to survive long enough for the rest of the world to catch up!

CHRIS BLISS

People / Different / Brand / Time / Experience

Chris Bliss left school at just 16, and became an apprentice in a factory that packaged soup. Now, decades later, he spearheads Liverpool ONE, the billion pound, 45 acre retail, leisure and residential project that has changed the face of the whole city. These days, rather than driving round in a van and worrying when the next payday is coming, Estate Director Chris oversees an operating budget of £10m at the development which has created 5,000 permanent jobs and won more than 60 awards. Here he tells us about his journey from teenage factory worker to being in charge of one of the most ambitious commercial and regeneration projects in the UK.

When I was a teenager, I loved the theatre. I was a behind-the-scenes guy, doing the lighting, building sets, that kind of thing. I was completely sold on a career in the theatre but was knocked off course slightly by some careers advice that told me to get a 'proper' job!

The proper job I got was as an apprentice for Nestle, as an engineer. I specialised in high speed packaging for soups – we were filling, sealing and printing one packet around every five seconds. It wasn't the theatre, or electrics, and it wasn't what I'd always dreamed of, but I look back on those days with a lot of affection, and also with the understanding now that they gave me a really solid base.

I learned about working hard; I learned about working shifts, I learned about paying a lot of attention to the quality of what you're doing. I learned how to get on with people from all walks of life and that you can enjoy a sense of camaraderie in the most unlikely of places. It might not sound it, but it was a lot of fun.

I might have a big title and a good job now, but I didn't go to university to learn the skills that got me here – in fact I left school when I was 16! That's something you don't hear so much of these days, but it worked for me.

I've always learned 'on the job', always been willing to change things up and use my knowledge in different ways. Every job I've ever had – including the false starts – have given me something I've used in later life. Nothing is wasted, even if it feels like it at the time.

After those early days as an apprentice, I did a bit of moving around. They wanted me to go and work in the office, which I thought was a very dangerous idea! I worked for a lift company for exactly two and a half days and for someone else. Then I went to college and got my qualifications as an electrician and started my own little business. I had always loved electrics, and couldn't think of anything I'd rather do then.

Sadly, this was the 80s. The recession started to take hold and things started to change. The work never dried up but the cash flow did.

Everything back then was done cash in hand, and once the cash stopped landing you were in trouble. I was married with a young family and a mortgage, and I had to think long and hard about what to do next.

It was a difficult period in my life, facing the challenges of having children - which can be hard in itself - and also trying to make a business work at the same time. I decided I had to face up to my responsibilities and start looking for a different path. It was what felt like the right decision for us all.

I think now, again with the marvellous power of hindsight, that everything worked out exactly the way it was supposed to. Without getting too deep and meaningful about fate or destiny, I do think that sometimes you look back and it all makes sense. Even the things you weren't sure about often lead on to something better; decisions you weren't completely happy with might result in a better opportunity.

For me, it was giving up the business and getting a job. That job was with a company called Equitable Life and I was a project manager, managing the building services, engineering projects, things like that. We were based in Aylesbury and every day I would see, from my window, a shopping centre being built in the town, Friars Square. And then, eventually, I saw a job advert for it, as Technical Services Manager.

I applied for, and got, that job, and it was a real turning point. I'd finally found a 'proper' job that I loved. It allowed me to combine my passion for all things technical – the electrics and engineering – with a managerial role, and with regular income. It was the start of everything for me, and led to me joining Grosvenor and ultimately becoming involved in Liverpool ONE.

Over the years, I've done different jobs, been promoted, been given different jobs and, effectively, risen up to where I am now. It's hard to put your finger on what exactly allows you to do that because some of it at least is based on other people's perceptions of you, not your own. But I did get an inkling of what one of my most appreciated qualities was when I was sitting next to a very senior Grosvenor person at a dinner once.

"Chris," he said, "I don't really understand what your job is. But I'm told that you are exceptionally good at doing all the shit that nobody else wants to do, and we're very grateful!"

That might be part of it, but there are definitely other characteristics at play too. It's sometimes hard to think about ourselves objectively, but one way I think about it is through brand. Working in the commercial sector like I do, and especially with Liverpool ONE, brand is very important. There's no reason not to also see yourself as a brand and ask the same questions: what is the Chris Bliss brand? What does he stand for? What do people associate him with? What qualities does his brand have? What are its key components? By looking at that, honestly, you'll perhaps get an idea of how other people see you.

> You need to know when to shut up and just think about something rather than talk about it.

That will be different for everybody, but I think my brand is made up of lots of different things. Loyalty. Integrity. Quality. Credibility. Being reliable. Not over-promising or under-delivering. Work rate. Tenacity. And creativity – that's so important. Perhaps it's my background, but I don't like taking 'no' for an answer. Decades ago, that might have related to a practical problem, something to do with engineering or lighting. I'd want to get to the bottom of a problem, take something apart, figure out how it worked and how to make it work better.

Now, it applies to other parts of my job as well, managing people, projects, finances, all the challenges that every day brings. I think, looking back, that one of the reasons I've worked for relatively few employers, and been with Grosvenor for so long, is that I am loyal and I am tenacious. I like to persevere and solve problems, and I like to see things through. I'm in it for the long haul!

There are always problems to solve, aren't there, in all walks of life? And you don't always get it right. The early days of building Liverpool ONE were hugely challenging. There were issues because of its massive scale, the sheer size of it, and the speed with which we were working. We were developing 45 acres of land in a city centre. We were dealing with different types of people, different agencies, different interests, finances and the practicalities of all those buildings, and making it all work.

If you only take marginal risks, or introduce marginal change, you'll only ever experience marginal success.

Of course there were days when I had steam coming out of my ears and wondered if I was going mad. Everyone develops their own coping strategies, and ways to deal with adversity or pressure. I'd say you need to grow a thicker skin. You need to know when to shut up and just think about something rather than talk about it. You need a sense of humour. You need to find a way to switch off – for me, it was learning to ski. I think physical activity – a sport, or walking, or learning something new – is a great safety valve. Believe me, while you're trying not to kill yourself on a ski slope, you're not worrying about work!

There are other things as well. Bear in mind, when you're building a team around you, how important they will be. If you surround yourself with a strong, resilient team, made up of strong, resilient people, it will take that pressure off. It will mean you have people to trust and rely on, and it will also reduce the risk of things going wrong.

You also need to be able communicate well. People who don't always have problems – if you can't clearly express your objectives or your expectations, you're heading for trouble. You need to have a certain level of self-confidence if you are going to inspire others. And you need to be able to think your way around risk.

This is a hard one, isn't it, risk? It's easy to over-think it. I believe that successful people have a dynamic approach to risk that is built into every day of their working lives. Nobody notices Mr Vanilla. If you only take marginal risks, or introduce marginal change, you'll only ever experience marginal success.

It's about combining calculated risk with your gut instinct, arming yourself with the facts, but also trusting your heart. It's also about timing – you might disagree with the way a client or your employer does something, for example, but there's no point alienating them by simply going maverick and changing everything. You need to be in tune with their views and their reasoning – and wait until the time is right to make the suggestions that will result in the change you are looking for. By all means push boundaries – but do it in the right way, at the right time.

> **It's business, it's not life or death.**

I think these days, we see a lot of young people – whether they are entrepreneurs or working for a company – who are too frightened to throw themselves into something 100%. They're too worried about questions like 'how will I ever afford my first car?', or 'how will I get on the property ladder?'. Perhaps it's to do with the current economic climate, but there is definitely a slightly nervous attitude.

I'd like to see more of them just having a go – it's business, it's not life or death. If you do happen to mess up, if it does all go horribly wrong, at worst you might lose your job – but it's not the end of the world. You'll have learned something, and you'll get another job and be even better!

I can see that with a certain level of experience, as there have definitely been a few twists and turns in my career. I've made mistakes and I've made choices and things have often felt hectic. But as a whole, it's worked out. That's a valuable lesson – that things work out in the end; something that experience teaches you. Stay calm in a crisis, because it will probably all be fine. Sleep on it, talk it out with a business friend, but don't assume that something going wrong will result in disaster.

I think experience has also taught me a lot about working with people. I met up with an old friend a while ago who I hadn't seen for 20- odd years, and he said I always used to do belligerence very well. Time has knocked some of those rough edges off me – I couldn't do my job as it is today if I was too belligerent, it just wouldn't work. So as well as our instincts and our work ethic, we need to allow time and experience to work its magic.

These days I get a great deal of satisfaction from my job. It's not easy, but I do love it. I think it took a while for it to sink in, how important Liverpool ONE has been. While we were building it, it was all about the nitty-gritty. About getting it done and making it work. Over the years, as it's grown, I've started to realise what a difference it's made to the city. You'd have to be blind to not see the divides in the area, the damage that multi-generational unemployment has done, the deprivation.

A project like this, that not only delivers commercially successful results for its investors but has also contributed hugely to the regeneration of the city, is incredibly satisfying.

That's become very important to me now, being involved in something that makes a difference. Looking back at those brand qualities – at what makes Chris Bliss – I think they work best when I'm involved with something I wholeheartedly believe in.

STEVE MORGAN, CBE

People / Money / Work Ethic / Passion / Opportunity

Digging sewers isn't the most glamorous of jobs by anybody's standards. The word drainage doesn't exactly scream success. But from these humble beginnings, Steve Morgan built Redrow plc – and became one of the most well-respected homebuilders in the UK. Here Steve reflects on the pitfalls and career turns which have helped him build a company with a turnover of £1.15bn, and which is responsible for more than 80,000 houses built to date. Having started his own business at just 21, he tells us about the need for passion, 100hour working weeks and some of the 'business commandments': Thou Shalt Be a Cheeky Bastard! And Thou Shalt Be Lucky!

I started out in this game pretty young. In fact, I started out in work in general when I was pretty young. As a kid, I worked on a bread delivery van when I was eight, had two paper rounds, and always had a job in the summer. I think that grafter in you is there from a very early age – it's a desire to improve your lot in life, and the work ethic to crack on with it and get it done.

I can't say I had a stable childhood. I went to nine different schools, lived in 10 different places. I was always the new kid – so I had to become a bit of a scrapper, both mentally and physically. It was tough, someone was always looking for trouble, looking to test me out. But it made me fearless, and self-reliant. It taught me skills and self-belief that I always used in business, and still do. It's best to learn early on how to use disadvantage to your advantage, rather than settling for being a victim.

So I worked hard, and I had bought my own house by the time I was 19. By 21 I was looking for opportunities to develop my own business. I didn't have huge amounts of life experience or skill – but what I did have was a very strong work ethic. I'm saying all of this because I think the first thing you need to realise, if you're looking to be successful in business, is that your work ethic has to be through the roof. It's the single most important thing.

People look at successful business men and they just see the trappings – the money, the respect. What isn't always so obvious on the surface is the work ethic. Like I say, mine started when I was young, and it carried on. It's still there. But, in the early days of running my own business, I was working long days, weekends, I was on sites all the time making sure everything was going the way it should. I was 21, and I was putting in 80-100 hour weeks at a time many kids my age were out enjoying themselves.

If you don't have that work ethic – if you're not willing to invest in yourself like that – then give up now. Find something else to do. Get a normal job, and don't frustrate yourself. You can forget all the rest if you don't have that, it's the basic building block. Look at what most people work in a week, and double those hours – are you willing to do that? Because that's what it takes.

When I started out in the 70s, I was digging sewers and drainage. I have a few commandments I think help you in business, and one of them is definitely 'thou shalt be a cheeky bastard'. I was a bit creative about my age and my qualifications and ended up working as a site foreman for a company which, soon after, decided it was going to withdraw from civil engineering.

On the day it announced it was closing it was also given a new contract. I said 'why don't I do this, as a sub-contractor'? That was a combination of being cheeky, and seeing an opportunity. And, if I'm honest, a little bit of luck.

The harder you work, the luckier you get.

Yes, I do believe in luck – maybe that's another one of my commandments, 'thou shalt be lucky' – but not in the way a lot of people do. I don't believe that luck is about buying a load of lottery tickets and hoping your numbers come up. I believe that luck is the way life has, of sometimes presenting you with opportunities. The skill is recognising them when they come – and most people are too busy plodding along through life to see them, or too scared to make the most of them.

Maybe it was because I was so young, maybe it was just my attitude, but I was always very driven, very keen to grasp opportunities. Having that self-belief, that confidence to think 'yeah, you know what, I can make this work' is absolutely vital. Don't be afraid to fail, to have a go.

I'm not saying you should be foolhardy, but if you give something your all, you'll be amazed at what the results can be. I've seen people over the years, very intelligent people with good ideas, but they've been too scared to take the leap. They've been paralysed by fear. If I hadn't been willing to take a chance on myself all those years ago, it would have been a very different story.

I also believe, though, that the harder you work, the luckier you get – and the more opportunities come in your direction. Using a football analogy - which I like to do! - look at Barcelona. It's not just that they're more skilled and talented than others. They're not mythical creatures. But they run 20% more than other teams – they work harder, they chase more. In business, you have to be Barcelona.

As well as the work ethic, and the self-belief, you have to be versatile. You have to be able to adapt to changing circumstances. Going back to when I was in my early 20s, and working in sewers and drainage, I got offered the opportunity to bid for a scheme for offices and warehousing. Now I'd never built anything above ground – it was totally new to me. But I had to adapt, to recognise the opportunity and have the right attitude to go for it, to change direction.

> It is the worst moments that define you, not the best ones.

All of this sounds like everything went perfectly, doesn't it? Like I worked hard and was lucky and everything progressed the way I wanted it to. That's not the entire story, though. Like anyone in business – like anyone in life – I've had some terrible times. Plenty of bad moments.

For me, a lot of those bad moments were all crammed into one year. I was very young, and it honestly felt like the crap was coming at me from all angles. These things often seem to come in batches, and you have to learn how to cope.

The year I'm talking about – the worst year of my entire life - work was drying up. I was struggling to keep all the guys I was employing in work, and I had to lay a few of them off. Laying good men off is awful. I was involved in a contract where I was losing money for the first time ever. Then, I had four car crashes in the space of six months, none of them my fault. My new car, my first ever brand new one, a TR7, got crushed beneath a load of tools and equipment in my garage. And, easily the worst of all, my brother was killed in a motorbike accident.

I just found myself thinking: what the hell is going on? What's going wrong? How do I get through all of this?

Everyone will react differently to times like that. But, if you want to survive, you have to find a way to cope. To not just sink into depression and give up, but to find a way out of the dark times, a way to stay hopeful and positive. Sometimes it is the worst moments that define you, not the best ones. The times when you dig deep and find the motivation to keep pushing through, no matter how terrible things seem. I can't tell anyone how to do that – it's something we all either find, or don't find, by ourselves.

A few weeks after my brother died I got offered a new contract, but I didn't have the money for materials. All my money was tied up in a side-project shipping luxury cars to the States, and I had no capital. On top of everything else that year, I learned a very important lesson: cash is vital. There's a saying in business that is completely true – turnover is vanity, profit is sanity, but cash is king.

So, I was feeling low, and needed a way out. That was a turning point – I could have given up then, but I didn't. I don't think many people could top that for a truly terrible year, but I kept trying, looking for the money I needed to take on that contract. In the end I found a bank that was willing to help me out, and the year after everything was completely different. The tide turned in my favour – but if I'd given up, the Redrow story would probably have finished right then.

It's hard for start-ups these days, for people running SMEs. It can be tough to get funding, to get people to invest in you, to get banks to lend you money. There are lots of problems to overcome. I think now, especially, you need those qualities in absolute bucket loads –

the work ethic, the ability to recognise opportunity, the confidence to take a risk, being adaptable, being determined and never giving up. Always trying to rise above adversity.

There's a certain type of person in whom you can see those qualities, and I always look out for them when I'm considering working with people or giving them a job. I look for certain mannerisms – a confident attitude, someone who comes in bright-eyed and bushy tailed, not slouching and moaning.

Sometimes, I even arrange meetings at really anti-social times just to see how people react – if they walk into the room and I know they've driven for hours to get there, and been up since the crack of dawn, and still seem enthusiastic and positive, I know they have the kind of attitude and ambition I can work with. They're people who have purpose, who will fight for what they want. If they grizzle and complain, and already seem tired and defeated, I'm not interested.

You also need to have a few other qualities that perhaps aren't quite so easy to define. If you look at the likes of real trailblazers, people such as Steve Jobs or Henry Ford, you see passion. You see people who are passionate about what they do – passionate about being the best, and about the product they are delivering. It's that passion, combined with the other qualities, which makes a successful entrepreneur. The entrepreneurship on its own isn't enough.

I still have that passion now. I look at what we are doing and I feel pride. If I don't feel pride I know something is wrong, and that we should have done better. I'm still constantly re-examining what we're doing, looking at ways to deliver a better product, to save money, to improve.

It's not just about building the business now, it's about a legacy as well, about place-making and contributing to a built environment. We're doing a Garden Village which I'm excited about. With age and financial comfort, you get the breathing space to do something a bit different. I get a huge thrill out of the Morgan Foundation, the biggest-giving charity in the North West.

I like to give back to the area I grew up in, and we've given away £30m since we started it. That's very rewarding, and a different way for me to use my passion and work ethic, benefiting others.

It's been a mad journey, this business, and my involvement in it. I stepped down as chairman in 2000, and came back in 2009, when it was in dire straits. That was a bit like starting again, and I'm proud of what we've done since – we've turned 600 people into 1800 people, and turned a £100m loss into £200m profit. I couldn't have done that without still feeling passionate.

I still love my work. I still find it exciting. Why? Because I care. I want us to be the best. There's time for golf in the next life!

PHIL MILLWARD

People / Work / Leader / Change / Relationships

Phil Millward started his working life as a 16-year-old school leaver, embarking on an apprenticeship at the Vauxhall Motors' factory in his home town, Ellesmere Port. During his 46-year career in the industry, Phil became renowned for working with the trade union movement to secure ground-breaking labour agreements that changed the face of car manufacturing in the UK. His work paved the way for General Motors' continued presence in Ellesmere Port, not only securing thousands of jobs but also influencing other business models across the country. By the time he retired from the company, Phil was the human resources director for General Motors UK and Ireland. Here he explains the importance of knowing someone's name, the power of positivity, and the dangers of the 'corporate psychopaths' who lurk in all big businesses.

My dad worked at the Shell refinery in Ellesmere Port, and the plan was that I was going to go to university and become an architect. Although he was great and supported me all the way, he hadn't wanted me to work 'on the tools', as he used to say.

But when I was 16, I made one of those decisions you make when you're very young, and decided instead to apply for an apprenticeship. I was offered two places, at Shell and at Vauxhall, and I chose Vauxhall because I liked cars, and I didn't want to work at the same place as my dad.

I'm sure I gave them a few sleepless nights at the time, but I don't regret any of it – it led on to a career that's not only been successful for me and my family, but has allowed me to make a real difference to the people I worked with, and the community I worked in. Vauxhall at Ellesmere Port recently celebrated its 50th anniversary, and I genuinely hope that some of my efforts there have set it up for its next 50.

Looking back, from being on the board of Vauxhall Motors all the way to being a teenager working there, the key to everything has been building relationships. People say this a lot, but actually doing it is a different matter.

In my 20s, I moved around Vauxhall, working in lots of different departments, in different jobs, and building up a treasure chest of experience. It didn't just teach me everything I needed to know about car manufacturing – it taught me everything I needed to know about people.

That was tested to the full when I was given the job of unit manager, general assembly – bit of a mouthful, but what it meant was that I was in charge of more than 5,000 people, including other managers who were older and more experienced than me. I was just this young whippersnapper barging in. I was a bit overwhelmed to start with, but eventually I just told myself I had to have some trust in the people who had given me the job – they'd seen some potential in me even when I was an apprentice, and I had to believe they knew what they were doing, even if I didn't always feel like I did!

This was the late 70s, early 80s, which was a very different era, but I believe the lessons I learned then, and the approaches I took, are still valid now. Labour relations were appalling, productivity was poor, and to call it a 'challenging' environment for a manager would be doing it a kindness. To be honest, it was like a war zone – all the different unions, the politics, the us-versus-them mentality.

> The thing about building relationships – you can't just build them when you need them.

Within an hour of walking into my new office, a union leader had walked in to tell me what was what, and put me in my place; to let me know how powerful they were, and basically say they could make my life a living hell. Well, I can be a little fiery myself, so that was an interesting start! But it did make me realise that the whole building relationships thing was more important then than ever.

Now, this is the thing about building relationships – you can't just build them when you need them. You can't think, 'well, I need this person to help me do this deal, so I'll show an interest and be nice to them'. That's not how it works. It has to start early and be consistent, and not just be about ways it can benefit you.

I realised that all these trade union leaders and members had basically been treated like the enemy, so that's what they'd become. If you show people disrespect, that's what you'll get in return. I decided to try and change all of that. I decided to try and bring them in, to share information, to empower them. The industry was facing a lot of challenges and I wanted them to understand those challenges because I realised that, instead of being the enemy, the unions could actually be part of the solution.

I saw it as my job to change the culture of mistrust and confrontation, and that wasn't easy. It didn't happen overnight. They were expecting the worst – and I gave them my best. I faced opposition on both sides, and it was a real risk. As well as trying to convince the unions we could work together, I had problems on the other side – some of the people above me in the organisation thought I was bonkers! They thought the unions were the enemy, that they had to be controlled. I had superiors accusing me of being in the unions' pocket, and the unions assuming I was a management flunky. I was in the middle, trying to change it all.

To be honest, if it hadn't worked out, it could have been a disaster. It was a real risk, but one I had thought through and believed in and was confident could make a huge difference to the way business was run. And, over time, those relationships were built, first locally, then regionally, then nationally. If you're tackling something like this, you need to be patient – don't rush it. Be willing to put the work in.

Don't get me wrong, it wasn't a cruise on the Love Boat – but it was a good working relationship. We didn't agree on everything, and sometimes I would back down, and sometimes they would. Compromise is the essence of successful negotiation, and it's important to remember if you're in potentially confrontational situations, that it's not necessarily about 'winning', or proving you're right. It's about finding a solution that suits everybody.

> You can read as many management manuals as you like, go on courses, but you simply don't get charisma from a textbook.

I was always committed to that, because I knew that's what was needed. I felt a real sense of engagement with the people who worked for Vauxhall, and wanted things to be good for them. They weren't just faceless employees – they were people. I made a point of knowing as many names as I could, and getting out on the shop floor as often as I could. I'd ask people about their family, chat about football. A successful leader needs to upgrade their visibility – be real.

Attitudes can change because of simple things like that. If you've got workers going home saying 'the boss came and had a chat to me today', and telling their mates, it makes them feel more valued and engaged. And that is invaluable in business – it's the person out there doing the job, day in day out, who has the most knowledge.

They're the experts, not you – and because of that, you need to listen to their views and their ideas. If you don't understand that, you're not worthy of being their leader.

It's also about being positive. People in senior positions, the executives, can talk about things like loyalty to the company, as though it's important – because they have choice. They can go and work somewhere else. Your average man or woman working in a car plant can't – they have no choice but to be loyal! But most of them will feel proud of working there, if you give them the right encouragement.

Someone once said to me, on the shop floor, that the staff had always been treated as though they didn't matter – as though they should hang up their brain at the gate, and pick it up on the way back home. That's no way to motivate someone, is it? Vauxhall – and a lot of other businesses – had a tendency to focus on the negative, to create an atmosphere of anxiety, of making people feel not quite good enough. The whole 'we've increased productivity by 5%, but why didn't we make it to 7%?' attitude.

This is sometimes a company-wide attitude, and sometimes it's the responsibility of a person you will find in all businesses – the corporate psychopath. The corporate psychopath cares about nothing but himself, and is committed only to his own CV. There is no 'we', only 'me'. They are power hungry and selfish and egotistical – never words that are applied to a good leader, and yet they always seem to exist, threading their way through organisations, without conscience, abusing trust. We've all met them.

The workforce isn't real to them. These people don't matter. And to succeed as a leader, you genuinely need to care. You need to want them on your side – your workforce is your most valuable asset. A leader who inspires pride in his workforce, who communicates powerfully, who motivates, is one who can master one of the most basic principles of business: your team needs to be working with you towards a common goal, not fighting you. You want them to feel invested in it, not as though it's the enemy.

So I focused on the positives and tried to create a more celebratory culture. I mean, if you're constantly being told the business is failing, that everything is a disaster, that you're falling short – would you want to get out of bed in the morning? Would you come into work full of enthusiasm and energy? No, none of us would – so part of being a leader is getting out there and sharing your energy! Make people feel good, make them proud.

> Without risk – calculated risk combined with your instincts – there will be no change.

Ordinary people can achieve extraordinary results – but they have to be motivated. There's nothing worse than a pessimistic and cynical manager, spreading doom and gloom.

Of course, some of this is simply down to personality. You can read as many management manuals as you like, go on courses, but you simply don't get charisma from a textbook. You can't learn empathy at university. You've either got it or you haven't.

When I was starting out, as a young apprentice, my managers saw something in me, and were willing to take a risk. They took a chance on me, and invested in me, and that taught me something – that you need to have what I call managerial courage. In business, not everything is clear cut, and you won't always be right. Sometimes you'll fail. But without risk – calculated risk combined with your instincts – there will be no change.

I'm not saying you shouldn't listen to other people, or be willing to admit when you're wrong, but managerial courage means sticking by your opinion and fighting your corner, if you genuinely feel it's the right course - like I had to with the unions. You need to be determined, and be prepared to take risks to reach your goals, and to have the courage to make decisions that other people, like the corporate psychopaths, want to tear down and pull apart.

I ended up as the director of human resources for GM in the UK and Ireland. I'm not a trained HR person, but I understand people, and I understand their psychology. I've worked with people from all walks of life, and I've seen what makes some stand out, and others sink.

If you're starting out in business, or in a new job, then be attentive. Listen, and be respectful. You might have a super-duper university degree, but the people you are working with might have invaluable experience – their own treasure chests of knowledge. Ask questions. Learn. Take your job seriously – and by that I mean your actual job, and not what it might contribute to your own CV. Work hard, do your best - even if it's not your dream job - because you're constantly evolving, and constantly adding to your own professional toolbox.

Never stop learning, and always remember to have some fun. You might have had the worst day in the world, but there is no situation that a bit of humour can't improve! Don't hold grudges, and if things go wrong, pick yourself up, dust yourself down, and move on. You'll survive, and you'll be better for it.

I look back now and feel so proud of everything we achieved at Vauxhall, especially at Ellesmere Port. A while ago, we knew that General Motors were going to close some of their bases for producing the Astra model. A lot of people expected that to be Ellesmere Port – but it wasn't. Plants in Germany and Belgium and Portugal went, and we didn't. We survived – and thousands of people kept their jobs. We were determined, we were courageous, and we had built a clear strategy and strong partnerships.

Vauxhall gave me a great career – but I like to think that I gave a lot back in return.

IAN MEADOWS, OBE, DL, FJMU

People / Mistakes / Family / Clients/ Responsibility

His plan as a youth was to 'paddle his own canoe and never come back'. Instead, Ian Meadows' life currents took him to Texaco, where he became their youngest sales manager by the time he was 23. His charismatic character and business acumen later saw him become a Deputy Lieutenant, Honorary Colonel and High Sheriff on Merseyside, after coming back to take over RS Clare, a veteran manufacturer (est. 1748). Ian – the fifth generation of his family at the helm - revived and transformed the company, expanding its international trade ties to the extent that it was honoured with the Queen's Award for Enterprise in 2011. Recently named in the London Stock Exchange's 1,000 Companies to Inspire Britain report, RS Clare is a niche market leader, exporting to more than 50 countries. Here Ian shares his views on the importance of management style, employee relations and focusing on the long-term sustainability of a business.

When I was younger, I didn't want to join the family business. I'd seen what it did to my father – all he did was work, he never had any fun and he used to come home reeking of tar. He was finished by the time he was 65, and dead by 69 – and that wasn't a fate I wanted for myself.

I also wanted to prove myself elsewhere, to show that if I did succeed, it wasn't because I was born with a silver spoon in my mouth. So I went to work for Texaco and, truth be told, at that stage I didn't intend to come back.

I was running the northern half of their Scottish retail operations by 26 and I learned a huge amount of valuable lessons. Being prepared to step out of my comfort zone was one of them, and I think that's as valuable a lesson now as it was then.

On one occasion, just as I started as a rep, I found that one of the Texaco petrol station tenants had gone bust. When I visited the site I found a ramshackle disaster of a place – right on the route to Gleneagles, where the company's President was coming to play golf the following day. I was told I had to sort it – so I did. In 24 hours the place was cleared up, painted and fully provisioned so he was completely unaware of the problem when he stopped off there the next day. The staff pulled together and I had to take responsibility for the business until I found another tenant.

I thrived at Texaco but, unfortunately, my father was diagnosed with cancer and I had to come back home. I took over as MD in 1979 but it took some getting used to, to change from a professional multi-national company to a small family business. It was like going back in time.

My Father and his peers were all dying off and little provision had been made for the future. The future was me! I'd been lumbered with a position I didn't really want. I remember when I first joined, the staff must have been told to call me 'Mr Ian'. I hated that – I was only 26, for goodness' sake!

But I hadn't only inherited the responsibility, I'd also inadvertently inherited a hierarchical management culture. Relations with staff and the union were both paternalistic and antagonistic. One department didn't talk to another, and trust was fragile. There was an atmosphere of blame and conflict. It was at the beginning of the 80s and Maggie Thatcher was making wholesale changes which were causing a lot of pain.

Initially I ran the firm as it was then being run which, with hindsight, was not helpful. I made mistakes without realising. I perpetuated the management style. It was all very hierarchical, old-fashioned, and it completely stifled staff enthusiasm. You can only criticise people so many times before they give up – until they stop using their initiative. If you stifle people's enthusiasm, you stifle the potential of the whole business.

The same can happen when businesses grow and become so dominated by processes and procedures that there's no room for creativity. Guides to decision-making become more formal. An unintended consequence is that initiative and judgement can take a back seat.

> You will do things wrong. Acknowledge that you are wrong, and have a clear plan for how you are going to put it right.

I had something of a 'Road to Damascus' experience when I was watching TV one night in 1989 and I saw Sir John Harvey Jones, the then Chairman of ICI talking about SMEs – he said that if they carried on as they were, trying to compete in the Common Market, yet operating on an Old Boys' Network, by the year 2000 they would all be gone. I realised he was right – and RS Clare was heading that way.

It was a moment of revelation for me and also one of clarity – I saw what I'd done wrong, saw what I needed to do to try to fix it, and decided to take action. That is essential in a leader – you will make mistakes. You will do things wrong. Acknowledge that you are wrong, and have a clear plan for how you are going to put it right.

The next day I went in to work and met all the employees in the works, on the shop floor. I stood on four pallets and told everyone what I was thinking – that our business was going to disappear if things didn't change. Most of all, I suspected, it was me who needed to change most! I asked them what kind of business they wanted to work for, and told them I genuinely wanted to work with them rather than fight them – but that we needed to pull together. A confidential survey showed that colleagues wanted delegation of responsibility and authority, better team working and two-way communication – just as did I.

At first, of course, there was suspicion, and some mistrust. People had had generations of conflict; they weren't going to believe me overnight. Trust takes a long time to build up. It's not just about what you say, but what you do – you need to have strong ethics, and to operate to high standards. Don't bullshit people. The man on the factory floor will spot that within a minute – the men at the bottom of the heap always recognise nonsense being talked a mile off!

I determined to share information with them openly and regularly and, gradually, people started to show interest in the business. Employees at all levels were gradually brought into the planning process and they began to want to contribute. Incentivising cemented that involvement.

Forward plans are communicated to everyone and we make sure everyone knows how they fit in and what their role is. Investing in training your staff and stretching them as people is worth every penny. Staff simply have to be trained to play their full part.

We share our progress throughout the year, reviewing performance and learning lessons from both good and bad experiences. You learn more from making mistakes, maybe more so than getting it right.

These days, if you walk around the place, you wouldn't recognise it compared with 25 years ago. We had a visitor from India recently and he was amazed at the fact that everybody wanted to talk to me. When I describe RS Clare as a family business, I mean everyone who works there – they are all part of the family.

People should get out of their comfort zone and live life. Make mistakes. Get some rough edges knocked off.

The changes at the business haven't just been about management culture – they've been about our brand, our products, and the way we work with clients. We are a niche firm, we don't need to be the biggest. We have a guiding principle that 25% of our business should never be more than three years old. That doesn't just keep us dynamic, it protects us from depending too much on one client base, or one collaboration.

We have a number of wholesale clients who we have been supplying grease to for decades. We try to make ourselves an extension of their supply chain rather than a supplier they just want to beat down on price; but there is always the awareness that, with clients like that, you can't be the master of your own destiny. All it takes is for someone you've never met in a faceless head office to decide to go in another direction, and you have a problem. That's a situation many businesses might find themselves in, and that's why we operate the 25% rule. R&D is absolutely key.

We focus on what we do well, and we stay diverse. Our brand name is essential – we aim to have a significant market share in our niche markets and we invest in R&D that can potentially (and lucratively) solve problems for clients. As we gain credibility, as we prove that 'it does what it says on the tin' and saves the client a lot of money, we can obtain worthwhile margins. We've achieved this in valve lubricants for the global upstream oil industry, for track lubrication in the UK and overseas, and for the deep sea wire rope market.

This isn't just relevant to our industry, but is something that applies to business in general. Keep moving forward, stay dynamic, control your processes, measure and review. Build a brand that's trusted, and a product that is more about quality than cost. Give people a reason to buy your cornflakes – or whatever it is you're selling – rather than somebody else's. I'm always looking for better ways to do things, and I think that's something you'll find in a lot of businessmen.

I sometimes think that I still don't know what I want to do with my life, and I recently turned 70! I have always been a very enthusiastic person, the people I work with know I'm straightforward, and I throw myself into things wholeheartedly. That kind of enthusiasm communicates itself to the staff – it's infectious!

But truth be told, I also lack self-confidence. I did some acting when I was younger and that helped to manage it but even now, with decades of experience in public speaking, I can still be crippled with nerves before the event. The secret is not to show it. I think, with hindsight, that I've taken on challenges just to prove to myself that I can conquer my personal doubts. Whatever I've done, I've tried hard to succeed, I've been determined to prove I could achieve – and that has brought some benefits. All you can do with a negative is try to turn it into a positive.

I'm very fallible but I've learned a lot over the years. I've learned to assume the person I am speaking to is more intelligent than I am, and to accord them respect. I've eventually learned to avoid coming to conclusions without having done my homework. I've learned to interview people at least three times before I make a decision to employ them as I am still prone to make snap judgements. I've learned that business is cyclical – there will always be highs and lows; an upward trend is what matters.

I really believe that people should get out of their comfort zone and live life. Make mistakes. Get some rough edges knocked off. Get some experience and learn from it.

And I've learned that, despite the fact that when I was young I didn't want this job, it has been much more of a privilege than a burden. I feel honoured to work with the people I work with, and I suspect that if you cut me in half, I'd have 'RS Clare' running through me like a stick of rock!

ANDREW COLLINGE

Relationships / Opportunities / Business / Work / Time

Andrew Collinge became a household name in the 1980s, when he regularly featured with his makeup artist wife, Liz, doing 'makeovers' on Richard and Judy's This Morning TV show. Watched by millions, the award-winning hairdresser was running a business empire that included a chain of successful salons, creating a product range and becoming one of the most famous stylists in the world. These days, the Collinge brand continues to grow and evolve, not only as a salon group, but as one of the most respected training providers to the industry. But what not many people know is that, back in the 70s, young Andrew had no interest in going into the family business; that he once washed Margaret Thatcher's hair, and that a lilac coloured perm changed everything for him. Here he tells us about the challenges of combining creativity with business, the importance of reinvention, and the need to work, work, and work some more.

Both my father and my grandfather had been hairdressers. My grandfather had a barber's shop and my Dad, Peter Collinge, became very successful in the world of competition hairdressing. That was something very much from a different era – it was very glamorous, there was a lot of travel, and he was competing against the likes of Vidal Sassoon.

The competition world was lucrative for my father and he was able to start his own salons and build the family business. My parents, though, had aspirations for me – and if you'd asked me as a child what I'd end up doing for a living, hairdressing would probably not have been on the list. As it turns out, I wasn't academically up to much, despite being sent to a good school!

In 1974, I ended up back at home, a bit clueless about what I wanted to do with my life. I think, in desperation, my dad said 'just do something – you can't just laze about!'. So I started going to one of his salons to help out. I was doing nothing special – sweeping the floor, making coffee, that kind of thing. But I really enjoyed the atmosphere there. It was a hot summer, I made lots of friends, and I loved the camaraderie of life in a salon. In fact, I enjoyed it so much I made the decision I was going to go into hairdressing myself.

I started working on the Wirral before moving to our Liverpool salon. It wasn't long before I started dabbling in competition hairdressing, like my dad. One of the first events I entered was the Guild of Hairdressers' Under 21 competition, getting through to the final in London. I permed my model's hair and coloured it lilac. Surprisingly I didn't win, but it did introduce me to the bright lights and lure of the capital city.

At the time you could say I had a cushy number, and in many ways I did. I worked for a secure family business, I was at home, with a car, having a good time. But I decided that if I was going to make my mark, I needed to build my own identity. I suppose this is one of those decisions that sometimes marks people out as being a bit different – deliberately choosing what seems to be a tougher path, because they just instinctively know it is the best one for them, and they have the confidence to take a risk and pursue it.

So I went for an interview and managed to get a position at the famous London salon Michaeljohn where I completed my apprenticeship. This was extremely glamorous. They did hair for A list stars such as Liz Taylor, Julie Andrews and Dustin Hoffman. I even got to wash Mrs Thatcher's hair – and she told me off for not voting!

My life, though, was anything but glamorous. It was extremely hard work, and on a trainee's wage I could only afford to live in a hostel. I could easily have not gone to London, stayed at home and had it easier, but I chose the hard way. I went from being established in my home town to basically starting again.

With hindsight, I'm able to say it paid off. I was able to build my own style, my own identity. It made me more determined, and helped me understand the industry so much better. Something inside me had told me it was the right thing to do, that I shouldn't be afraid to try. I'm not saying I didn't have any wobbles – we all do. You have those moments where you start to doubt yourself, wonder if you've made the right choices, if you'll ever achieve your goals.

Well, all I can say is that you learn a lot about yourself and lot about other people and a lot about life while you are washing hair. I also had the good fortune of meeting my wife, Liz, while I was down in London.

By 1982, I made another one of those decisions that on the surface seemed a bit mad – to come back to Liverpool at a time when the city was going through challenging times, to say the least. I was leaving a very well respected position at Michaeljohn – as Artistic Director I represented them at some of the world's leading trade shows, demonstrating the latest trends in hairdressing in front of international audiences – but, again, I knew that leaving the comfortable situation and taking this risk was right for me – for us, as we also wanted to start a family. Coming back to Liverpool in the 1980s seemed an odd decision on the face of it but, again, it worked out.

If there is one thing I've learned it is to trust your instincts, and also that you don't know where opportunities are going to come from, or when they are going to come. You have to constantly work, work and work some more – get yourself out there, get known, keep trying. At the trade shows, make contacts, network, get your name talked about.

It was being creative, and working hard, that led to those opportunities – the competitions, the awards, the profile-building, the image. It all helps get you noticed – and once you have been noticed, there are more opportunities. Getting your name out there definitely pays off – for us, when the call came from the Richard and Judy team on the daytime TV show This Morning.

> You have to stay relevant, be willing to reinvent, and never become complacent.

Liz and I started on the show at the very beginning, and it has since turned out to be one of the most popular shows on television. We ended up appearing for 10 years on the show and completed more than 500 makeovers.

It was hard work – we'd do the show in the morning and be back in the salon an hour later, as well as dealing with the growing business aspect of things. But it was definitely worth it and really changed everything.

The publicity and public awareness from appearing regularly on network TV was huge, and resulted in Liz and I having the opportunity to work on our own product lines. We both developed excellent working relationships with much bigger partners in the hair and beauty industry, resulting in ranges selling under our names doing well in both the UK and internationally.

Running a business takes drive and determination and sacrifice. I think one of the key things is having attainable goals but also learning to deal with uncertainty. I have found, in my career, no two days have ever been the same, and creating hairstyles and working on new techniques was only one part of the equation; the rest was the business side of things.

I have loved my job, but have learned with experience. At the start, I tended to say 'yes' to too many things – it's worth always taking a moment to ask yourself what your brand is; what you stand for, whether there is a time to go for quality rather than quantity. How will what you are doing affect your relationships? Because that's what it's all about – relationships with customers, with staff, with partners. You always need to treat your clients as individuals, and your staff as the precious things they are – good relationships lead to longevity, low staff turnover, and more security.

Having said that, of course, in any business, you can never be 100% secure. There is a lot of responsibility – we have a lot of employees, a reputation, and a position in the community. But, on the flipside, nothing gives you more satisfaction than seeing those employees do well, or seeing someone who joined you at 16 grow in confidence and go on to build a successful career and life. We even have the children of original staff working with us.

Hairdressing is a fast-moving business; things change quickly, and you have to be able to change with it. We have continued to evolve. You have to stay relevant, be willing to reinvent, and never become complacent. Our training business is incredibly successful and very important to us. We now have our own product range, CO by Andrew Collinge, that we completely own, which feels very rewarding.

Moving forward, I'm now concentrating my time on a creative role and have passed on the running of the business to my son, Charlie. He's not a hairdresser – his background is in design. He has the ability to pay fantastic attention to detail and is introducing exciting new opportunities into the business. I'm very proud of what he's achieving, and seeing what he's capable of is an absolute revelation. It's very reassuring to know the company is in such safe hands and entering a fourth generation.

MAX STEINBERG, CBE

People / Team / Believe / Honesty/ Environment

The aftermath of the Toxteth riots of 1981 saw a young Max Steinberg working alongside the Environment Minister Michael Heseltine in an attempt to attract private investment to a damaged Liverpool. Together, they struggled through dark days to finally persuade a handful of financiers to climb aboard a tour bus and visit a city that was socially and economically at a very low point. Thirty three years later, he was chairing the UK's first International Festival for Business, and welcoming over 68,000 delegates from 92 countries to Merseyside in 2014 and then repeated the same success in 2016. Here the chief executive of the economic development company Liverpool Vision and chairman of the IFB shares his views on business culture, leadership and how to create an environment which allows commerce to thrive.

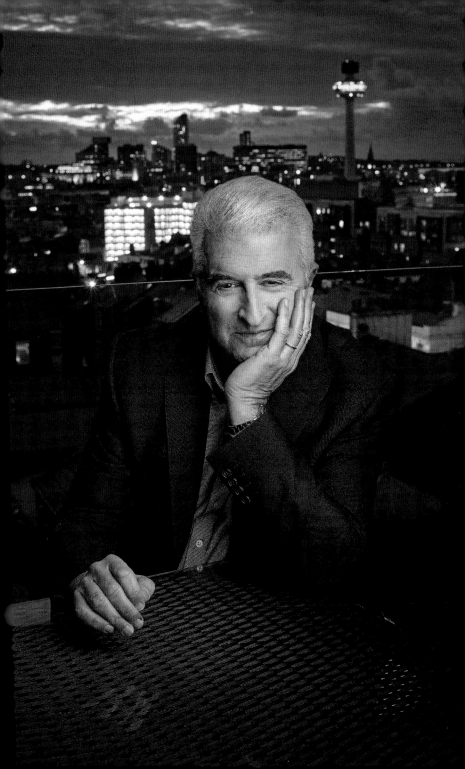

In some ways, I have been lucky in my career – I fell into it by accident, working for the council while I was waiting to go and study law. I soon realised that I wanted to stay in and around government, that this was an environment where I believed I could make a difference and really achieve something. I was able, in the earlier days of my career, to work on some great schemes, such as the Anglican Cathedral Precinct, Project Rosemary and the Eldonian Village – major regeneration projects where Liverpool was leading the way.

> One of the best things you can do in business is to look, listen and learn from others.

I was also able to work with inspiring people like Lord Heseltine, Sir Christopher Benson and Sir Brian Pearse, and I still believe, to this day, that one of the best things you can do in business is to look, listen and learn from others.

Having worked with communities and business for a number of decades, I have definitely noticed a few common factors in those who succeed as entrepreneurs, and those who become great leaders.

They all have drive. They have real ambition to make a change, to achieve. They have pride, in a job well done, a project completed, or a goal reached. They have passion for what they are doing, a true belief in themselves and what they are trying to do, and in their ability to succeed. They are usually naturally optimistic. Optimism needs to be part of your approach – you have to believe that things can change for the better. If you don't have that, you probably won't succeed because you don't have the strength to bounce back from the setbacks which will inevitably come.

For me, there are some additional ingredients, especially if you are leading a team. You need to genuinely value and care about people – your workforce is the best and most important asset you have.

You also need a sense of humour. My dad was a doctor, and he used to come home from work with some, often terrible, jokes because people told them to him, and he shared them with other patients to try and alleviate difficult situations. A bit of banter and some laughter can go a long way to making everything feel more manageable. Being able to lift the mood, even if it's just with perhaps a lame joke that breaks the ice, is essential.

> When things go wrong, people don't say they're sorry often enough.

A big part of working in a business environment – in fact, a big part of life – is recognising that you can't control everything. You can work and work and work, have all the drive and ambition in the world, but sometimes things simply don't work out. There is only so much you can do; things will go wrong, you will make mistakes, others around you will make mistakes. You have to learn how to cope with those disappointments, and learn from them. It's human nature to worry and become anxious about things we can't control, but if you let it take over, you will lose your sense of direction, your optimism, your creativity, and your passion.

The flip side of that is learning to build the right business; work relationships and partnerships that minimise that feeling of being 'just one person'. Business is all about building professional relationships which are based on trust, honesty and respect – accepting that yes, we all want to get something out of the relationship, but going about it in a mutually beneficial way. Treat everyone with respect and dignity, and don't be afraid to say sorry if you're wrong. When things go wrong, people don't say they're sorry often enough.

Honesty is vital in everything. If you are not honest, if you're found to be covering something up, you lose your credibility. People will stop believing in you, and how can you expect to lead a team, or inspire people to share your vision, if they don't believe in you? Honesty isn't always the easy option, sometimes there are unpleasant truths that need to be dealt with.

When I became chief executive of Liverpool Vision, it was a great team, but because of budget pressures we needed to make some reductions. It's not a pleasant or easy thing to have to tell people, and there may be very few ways to lessen the impact, but I can say that everyone who was affected by that was dealt with honesty and dignity. There is no use shying away from the tough decisions, but you can handle the process in such a way that people feel respected.

Working with and inspiring a team of people is something which partly comes naturally to me – I do believe some people have more self-confidence than others, for whatever reason. But I also believe that a lot of skills can be learned: how to build professional relationships, sharing ambitions in a way which inspires the people around you, displaying loyalty and tenacity in a way which encourages your team to develop those qualities themselves.

I don't think you necessarily get all of this from formal training alone, but also by watching and absorbing what you see around you, and by simple experience. As you go through life, you build up more skills, more abilities, more reflexes. You go through situations where perhaps you don't react as well as you would have liked, and you learn from that, and you're ready the next time. You start to be able to blend judgement with experience and making the right decision, but sometimes you only get there – in part - by making the wrong calls.

That said, sometimes you need to be bold. You need to take risks to make something different happen.

I once worked in an area where there had been a lot of civil disturbance – hate crimes, people from different communities living what was termed 'parallel lives', the rise of the BNP, tension on the streets, racist daubings, and knife crime. One of the ways I decided to try and tackle that was by organising a number of mediation meetings between community leaders from all sectors. To start with, people stood up and literally shouted at each other, saying some very unfortunate things, and it looked as though it was going to be a disaster.

But things did settle down, and eventually we achieved something. I'd had no idea going in whether it was going to work or not – but the daubings, the knife crime and the hate crime, it did all reduce. Being bold and being willing to take a risk are essential in business, and creating a thriving economic environment. In 2010, we led a Liverpool delegation to the Shanghai EXPO. At the time, there was a lot of criticism. It was considered to be an expensive venture and certain critics thought we'd fall flat on our faces. In fact, the opposite was true – 770,000 people visited our pavilion, and listening to others talk about Liverpool with such passion and belief inspired us to reach further.

When we came back, we made a bid to the Kauffman Foundation to host a highly prestigious event called the Global Entrepreneurship Congress – this was a gamble but we were on something of a high after Shanghai. We won, and it was a huge success. Richard Branson was part of it, and it very much put us on the global business map.

Later in 2014, in the lead up to the first International Festival for Business, we were still encountering critics saying 'why isn't this in London?' But by making bold decisions on behalf of Liverpool, we were making a statement. We were saying – to business people here, and around the world – that Liverpool is a global business city. And if business prospers, the wider community will prosper.

Those situations worked out and worked out well, but not everything does, all of the time. It's vital to remember that nothing is perfect - perfection doesn't exist, it's that simple. You do the best you can, and sometimes you win, sometimes you lose, but you always need to learn.

I'd also say to anyone embarking on a business career, or with a high pressure job, that it's very important to have a life outside it. I am lucky enough to have a beautiful wife and two children, who are now grown up. Having a strong family life has meant that I have always had an escape hatch, a completely different environment, with completely different priorities, that I could step back into to balance it all out. I could leave work behind and concentrate on being a husband and a dad as well.

It's all part of understanding that although it's important to be ambitious, and to pursue success, success comes to us in many different ways.

Staff / People / Family / Customers / Survive

After leaving Shrewsbury school in the late 1960s, Nicholas Wainwright joined his family business as it seemed like a natural path. He started by learning the business from the bottom up, wrapping parcels and polishing silver, but his growing experience soon turned into a lifelong passion for his work and the business. This may not be such a surprise when that family business is Boodles, one of the most respected jewellery designers in the world - famed for its Million Pound Necklace, sourcing diamonds worth millions, and having its jewellery included in the Victoria and Albert Museum's permanent collection. Now, Nicholas heads the company as creative director and chairman, helping it compete with the 'big boys' of international fine jewellery and keeping a close eye on the ever-changing styles in the industry. Through the company's association with top-level sporting and social events, and celebrity clientele, Boodles has become almost unrecognisable from its previous life. Here the man renowned for wearing pink socks and ties which match its brand colours talks us through the processes behind that transformation, the importance of embracing change, and why he always carries a notebook and pen.

I left school back in the days when not everybody automatically went to university. Certainly, if you had a decent family business to go into, that's what you did.

When I started working at Boodles, I was pretty green. I wasn't an academic, I only had one and a half A-levels and, at that stage in my life, it's not as though I was desperate to join the jewellery business – that was simply the route I was following, because it was there for me.

It didn't take me long, though, to realise that I loved it – that I loved it with an absolute passion; not just the work but the company, the product, the people, everything about it. I'm so very fortunate handling beautiful jewellery for two or three hours a day every day – so much more interesting than running a ball bearing factory.

After that, I had to learn my trade. This is something that can't be underestimated because, while there might be certain rules or guidance which can apply to business in general, if you are specialising in one type of business, then make it your business, know it inside out, everything about it. You owe that to yourself, and to the people who will be working with you and for you.

That's what I did. I spent several years working on the bench making jewellery in London, living in Geneva with watch companies, studying to be a qualified gemologist, doing retail business courses, travelling, getting to understand every technical aspect of what we did and of how the jewellery business operated.

My drive was based on my passion for what I was doing. Partly, it was based on heritage – it was in my blood - and partly I think, and I'm sure this is not uncommon in business people, it was also based on a very strong desire to succeed. Boodles had been established for more than 200 years; I didn't want to be the one who mucked it all up. There was an element of fear of failure, and that helped my focus. I was determined that our business wouldn't go bust, wouldn't fail, wouldn't get sold and that it would be preserved for future generations.

I work very closely with my brother Michael who is now managing director, my son Jody who buys all our beautiful diamonds and my nephew James who oversees all our marketing. We had to make some serious changes, and I say 'we' because it was very much a family decision. Boodles is a family business and we make sure we communicate well, we get on, and we have fun. We share decision-making – at our last directors meeting we actually spent two days sitting around a swimming pool in Dubai in our swimming trunks, but not having time for a swim. We enjoy each other's company, we work well together, we never vote and never fall out – whether it is your family or not, it is essential to get on well with others in business, to listen to their opinions, to simply work together for a common goal.

> It's not a matter of being able to see the future, but it is a matter of having a vision and the determination to see it through.

Change, in a long-established family business like ours, can be a daunting prospect. You have to be able to understand and respond to the changes going on around you. It's not a matter of being able to see the future, but it is a matter of having a vision and the determination to see it through.

Twenty-five years ago, we were a solid, well-respected county jewellers. We sold a lot of nice silver, clocks and watches – but times were changing. We felt that if we wanted to succeed where others failed, to stay alive and stay profitable, we also had to move with the times. So we had to focus on the areas with the most potential to survive and, for us, that was fine jewellery. We wanted to build our own Boodles brand, to focus on high-quality design, on amazing jewellery. We started with one designer and now have five in our design studio, and apart from Patek Philippe watches, we design and make everything we sell in our stores.

That wasn't as simple a process as it sounds. As we dropped so many product ranges, we lost some customers – but ultimately, we gained others and found a way to survive. If I look at my old address book from all those years ago, many of the people who were in the same business as Boodles went under. Those names simply no longer exist – they fell victim to the changing way that people shop.

We had to change, to adapt, in order to survive. It was a risk, but one we all agreed on: to up our game and compete with the very best in the world. Once you make the decision to compete with the likes of Cartier, you've set the bar very high for yourself – but we knew it was the right thing to do.

I was determined to build up the Boodles brand, not only for myself, but for the family, the future and for the people who work for us and with us. Running a business comes with a lot of responsibility. You can understand that in theory, but until you are there – until you are the one who has been given that responsibility – you don't truly appreciate it.

All businesses have their own different individual needs, but there are some rules which apply to us all. You need to stay on your toes. Don't get complacent, don't assume that just because doing something a certain way has worked for 20 years, it always will. Things change – you have to be alert to it, and able to respond to it.

You need to pay attention to what your competitors are doing, although we never ever copy them. Look at what is working for them, and what you can learn from that. As in the Olympics, we always aim to win the gold medal, not the bronze or fourth place.

To stay in business for more than 200 years one can never afford to take too many risks. We have survived through wars, recessions and depressions. You will never survive with huge overdrafts and masses of debt. Don't over-expand before you know you are ready. Don't take your eye off the ball, don't over extend and take too many risks.

Ten years ago we were looking to open another store and we visited Leeds, Edinburgh and Glasgow on a wet day in February. Then we went to Dublin, and it happened to be glorious sunshine, and we

As in the Olympics, we always aim to win the gold, not the bronze or fourth place.

thought 'oh yes, this is the place'. The problem was, of course, we hadn't really thought it through – we'd let our hearts rule our heads and not done enough research.

It was a massive challenge, as Ireland has a different currency, a different legal system, and of course an economy which soon afterwards took a nosedive. We completely under-estimated the situation which would be facing us – and we learned from it. Thanks to 10 years' of very hard work, the Boodles store in Dublin is now running well, is very profitable and we are confident about the future. The lesson is you have to be sensible about the risks you take.

One of our most important challenges is our relationships with customers, and ensuring they are given the 'Boodles experience'. Our customers get a whole experience from their relationship with us. It's very personal – we get to know them, to like them, we want to gain their confidence and make them happy.

That is a subtle and important process – it involves our stores and how they look; our marketing and branding, the way we align ourselves through sponsorship; the product, and, of course, our staff – expert staff who all contribute to that customer experience. If even one of those ingredients is missing, things can come tumbling down.

We pay great attention to trends, to design, to key elements like shop fitting and PR. We may look as though we are punching above our weight in terms of size, and our largest international plc competitors have much deeper pockets than Boodles, but we still see ourselves as first division, not second – and I believe our customers see us that way too. We have examined every aspect of our business – from product to price – but ultimately, you also need to simply get those relationships with customers right.

It's important to look after your staff. We try and support them in their own career ambitions. We treat them well, we pay them as well as we possibly can, and do everything to keep our best staff. It makes good sense to keep your best staff. Boodles is a philanthropic company and we encourage our staff to be the same, giving each of them an annual charity budget. We encourage them to use it and try to be generous. We try not to forget that the world outside of fine jewellery can be very, very different to our world.

I had the importance of integrity driven into me by my father throughout my life. He would always say that you don't build anything long term by sailing close to the wind. Your reputation is invaluable. You need to pay your bills on time, do what you say you're going to do, be efficient – he used to always carry a notebook and pen, and I still think that's a good idea now. I still make notes for everything on my daily pink card.

Now, looking back on my career and knowing that the next generation is in a position to continue to build, I can see the importance of all these things. One thing I can say is that I've never wanted to retire or to sell the business. At 68 I still love my work, even though the Test Match will probably be on view in my office.

I am still passionate about what I do, and I think that is so important, because if you don't believe in what you are doing, how can you expect anybody else to.

IAN AND NEILL BRIGGS

Learn / Attitude / Money / Decisions / Balance

As teenagers, many young people might dream of owning the supercar which features on the poster on their bedroom wall. But not many teenagers grow up to say that they build cars which end up on the posters. After years of working with major automotive brands like Porsche, Mercedes and Bentley, brothers Ian and Neill Briggs can still look at the posters of McLarens, Paganis and Lamborghinis - but these days they spend their time making a car which could rival them on the road and on a track. The founders of Briggs Automotive Company (BAC) now build some of the fastest road legal cars in the world. However, while the world of supercars might look exciting on the surface, producing their first car, Top Gear STIG's Car of the Year, the Mono, was anything but glamorous. It involved working more hours than sleeping, basically living in a big shed, and getting lost on the way to test drives. Now they export the Mono – the world's first road legal single-seater car – all over the globe, and have a dedicated following in the world of elite motoring. Here they tell us about their early challenges, learning to delegate, and how running a business feels like climbing a mountain.

We were both working as freelancers when we made the decision to do this. Neither of us was in a 9-5 job, we were in situations where we had to be entrepreneurial in different ways – working as a consultant keeps you on your toes. You're only as good as your last piece of work, and you're judged by your performance. It gives you a real drive to do well – and it means you're always looking for interesting new projects, meeting new people, adapting to new situations.

> You're only as good as your last piece of work.

It also meant that between us we had a lot of experience – we had the expertise, we had the right attitude, we knew that we could do this. Together, we could tackle any part of the car. Both of us had passed the stage where we wanted to work to someone else's brief. We didn't want to help make other people's ideas become a reality; we wanted to make our own decisions. Of course it was a risk – but we were both driven to do it.

The early days were mainly research and development, but eventually we went from a blank sheet of paper to a car. It wasn't simple – but nothing in life, or business, ever is. Other people looking in from the outside might think that things had moved quickly, certainly within our industry, but to us it sometimes felt painfully slow, and we had to learn a lot of patience. We had to constantly reset our own expectations.

In fact, we had to learn a lot of things. In those days, we were pretty much doing everything – we were the grease monkeys and the drivers, but we were also the bosses and the directors. To say that we were multi-tasking is putting it mildly.

Everyone has certain strengths and weaknesses, things they are better at than others, but when you start out you are often in a position where you just have to get on with things. It's a very steep learning curve, and at times it did feel crazy.

There were no weekends off, we were pulling all-nighters, and it all felt a bit unreal. We had to create more hours in our days, so we developed a kind of shift pattern; sometimes we'd just nod at each other as one arrived and one left. It was hectic – things like driving through the night and getting lost because of a cheap sat nav on the way to our Top Gear test drive, or driving 36 hours to Malaga.

If you're not prepared to put that level of effort in to your business, you should probably look for something else. Some people are happy doing their job and getting their salary, and there's nothing wrong with that, but it's not us. We had to put literally every moment we had into this to even get started. That type of lifestyle takes its toll, and it's all-consuming, but for us it was worth it. We had this vision of what we wanted to create: a car that would give people the best driving experience of their lives. A car that, while they were driving it, would make them forget about their own problems.

Nobody is lucky enough or good enough to get everything right the first time.

We put our hearts and souls into it – as well as all our time, and energy and money. It's not for the faint-hearted, and there were knocks. But you need to learn how to cope with those. It's the same for all business leaders. The likes of Steve Jobs and Richard Branson all had knocks in their professional life. It's not like you just open a record shop and become a billionaire – these are people who have had their share of business traumas. As many things will go wrong as right; you need to go into that with your eyes wide open, and with the right attitude. You need to be self-critical and open to constructive criticism from others.

The business aspect of things, as much as the car, was like a prototype we were working on – we are always needing to make tweaks, refinements, change things up. Nobody is lucky enough or good enough to get everything right the first time.

One of the things that we've learned along the way is that as soon as you learn something, you need to learn something else! It's an on-going journey. We didn't start this with the aim of creating a manufacturing business which exports all over the world – we just wanted to create a great car. To start with, there were areas we were unsure of and as your business grows, so does your need to understand how that aspect of your world works. As you get bigger, you need to be thinking about things like recruitment, procurement, HR, finance departments, all the stuff that we didn't consider quite as much when we started out.

You need to figure out when to delegate. In the early days, you don't have much choice, you just get on with it. But as the workload increases, you have to be realistic – you can't do everything yourself, and you shouldn't even try. You have to look at the balance: do you need to take someone on to do that thing for you? Can someone else do it better? Where are your own talents and skills best used and where would it make sense to get help?

That's not always an easy balance, especially when your business is constantly evolving at the pace ours has evolved. We had to fight like dogs to get to the stage where we even had a car on show, but then we realised that this was just the beginning – that the interest was there, that the next stage was going to be huge. Ours is a very fast-moving industry; there is always new technology, new design trends, changes in the market, new aims to go for. As a result, the goalposts are always moving and we can never sit still.

You have to make big decisions as things change. We had to relocate – from a big shed in Cheshire to a bigger and posher shed in Liverpool. You have to invest in people. You have to give some serious thought to your finances: do you struggle through or do you take your product out and look for investors, giving up an element of control? Those decisions are not easy, and depend on your attitude, your goals and the growth rate of your business. By hook or by crook we managed, but it wasn't by any means easy.

For us, it was also about balancing our passion for what we were doing with the need for financial success. We are ambitious, and we have surrounded ourselves with talented and creative employees who love their work and share our vision. For all of this to work, there has to be that balance between the creativity and the financial. It's not just about money – in fact for us it is about so much more; if it was just about money, there are far less stressful ways to go about it. But we also live in the real world, and it's important to not lose sight of that.

A vital element of everything we do revolves around relationships. We know our customers incredibly well. We have a great relationship with our team, with our suppliers, partners and collaborators. You need to get out there – do the networking, put the hours in meeting people and getting your name known. The people you meet that way might not be immediately useful to you, but at some point down the line, they will.

You have to communicate and present yourself well, make a good impression and be able to back it up with a good performance. People need to trust you and respect your abilities, and if you don't have a track record because you are just starting out, that will be based on the way you come across and your attitude.

One thing we've definitely both noticed is that there is no finishing line – you never get to the point where you think, phew, we've made it! You are always learning, always meeting challenges and always developing new goals.

It's a bit like mountain climbing in the Himalayas or something – you fight and fight to get to the top of the peak, and feel a momentary sense of relief, but then you look ahead and there are mountains as far as the eye can see!

NICK EARLAM

People / Learn / Family / Time / Team

Quite unconventionally, after A-levels Nick Earlam chose to go into cotton trading rather than to university. Having gained experience as an apprentice and later as head of the trading division in a cotton trading company, he sold his house, cashed in his life insurance policy, borrowed some money from his mother and started his own business. The early years were tough, with 20-hour working days and £2,000 profit against £200,000 overheads – but now Nick is a leading figure in the international cotton trade, whose company, Plexus Cotton, turns over more than half a billion dollars annually, and employs thousands of people in its global operations. Here Nick talks about the importance of embracing change, taking responsibilities seriously, and not wasting time on corporate politics.

I was 32 when I started my own business, and I was bullish – everything was based around my self-belief. You need that to start off with, to get anywhere at all. Even though I invested all my money in it, and the risk looked huge from the outside, it just felt totally right to me. I sold up everything to get it going, and was lucky enough to have supportive family and friends, but I never doubted that I was heading in the right direction.

The early days were very hard, and you have to be prepared for that. A lot of things in the world have changed since then, the whole way we do business has changed, but that truth remains the same – you have to believe in yourself, and you have to be willing to work, work and work some more.

I suppose, back then, I was operating as much by instinct as knowledge, but it didn't take me long to realise the importance of doing your homework. You have to do the research and pay attention to the maths, the trends and the reality of your business situation. Yes, you need to be courageous and willing to take on the world, but that will only get you so far if you don't have the foundations and fundamentals in place.

One of those fundamentals is working with people you trust. Without good allies, you simply will not succeed. This is something I've learned along the way – you shouldn't surround yourself with 'yes men'. My first board used to agree with everything I said and then criticise me behind my back. That's not good for a whole variety of reasons, mainly because you then lose the fresh ideas and perspective that your team should be bringing to you. Business is like a football team – you can work and practice, but you also always need to be looking for fresh blood, new talent.

Building relationships – with customers, employees, everyone you come into contact with – is essential. Doing that well comes with time, and with being fair and acting in other people's interests, not just your own. You want to be working with people towards a mutual objective, with people who will stick with you through thick and thin. You need people to be working in an environment where they are not afraid to express their opinion, even if it is different to yours.

Over the years, I've noticed that the great business leaders are all good listeners. They're not afraid to hear people's opinions. They are often very humble. It is people like that who inspire and lead, not the pompous ones full of their own self-importance. Great business leaders have usually been to hell and back, and take nothing for granted. No matter how successful you are, you're just a grain of sand in the ultimate scheme of things.

If you have respect for other people, you are always open to learning from them and their experiences. Having travelled the world, it comes as no surprise to me that in places such as China, India and Africa, their mentality is based around huge respect for their elders, and placing them at the pinnacle of the family. Again, these are people who have been through it all, and have wisdom and guidance to share.

You definitely learn some of this as you progress through your life and your career. I believe that I had some natural leadership skills - in sports for example – but I couldn't have gone off and become a nuclear scientist. We all have different strengths and weaknesses, and it's important to appreciate what they are. Anybody who builds something – a business, a career, a family – is a complex blend of natural abilities, faults and experience.

In business, it can't be all about what you can take, it has to be about what you can give back.

I think another essential attribute is the willingness to accept change, to be able to adapt and embrace progression. The world is a vastly different place than it was in 1990 when I started the business. Facebook, Airbnb, WhatsApp – these and many others reflect the dizzying revolution we've seen. These days, you no longer have to be in an office, you can work in a yurt in Mongolia with a laptop and a phone.

That means a lot of change – and all you can do is adapt to it. Years ago, for example, nobody would have understood the complex supply chain which resulted in an item of clothing being sold in John Lewis or some other department store. Now, everything is very transparent so you need to ensure that your brand, your relationships, your actions and ethics are up to that kind of scrutiny. Embrace it and work with it, don't cling on to your old ways because you are afraid of the new. For us, that has involved changing our business model completely.

In the same way that you cope with change, you have to cope with adversity. There are masses of instances in my career where things have gone wrong. Six months into my business, I had a 10,000 tonne shipment of cotton damaged at sea and it took me nine months to be paid out by the insurance company. We also had a legal case in the States that we had to fight for four years before we won it.

Trials and tribulations like these will happen to any business person, and at the time they can feel crushing. But this is where you learn, and this is what makes you stronger. The good times take care of themselves – it is the hard times where you need all your wits about you, all your determination, all your creativity and all the support of your team.

Again, in the early days, you might not think you can work through some of these challenges – but you can. You will. As you get older and more experienced, you will learn to absorb pressure differently. When you're in your 50s, it's a bit more 'been there, done that, got the T-shirt'! Adversity can enrich you and when times are tough, when you're working so hard just to keep your head above water, that's when you learn the most.

> We come into this world with nothing, and we leave with nothing – what matters is enriching the world as you journey through it.

Over the years, I've also learned to be wary of a few things. Pride can trip you up, if it stops you seeing the bigger picture and stops you admitting that you are wrong. Great leaders, whether that's corporate or personal, have the ability to see when they are wrong – without that you are a disaster waiting to happen!

It's the same with corporate politics. It's a huge waste of time – nothing chews into your day like game-playing. You need to start to recognise the people who simply want to get the job done, and the people who just want to posture and talk a good game. The latter to be avoided at all costs!

For me, another vital part of the business equation, especially in my industry, has been responsibility. In business, it can't be all about what you can take, it has to be about what you can give back as well. That might be in terms of the way you treat your employees, it might be about investing in communities, fair business practices and environmental sustainability.

These things aren't just boxes to be ticked for CSR – they matter. I was brought up in a way that placed great value on social justice; I was raised to be fair and to not do things I knew I wouldn't be proud of. You need to combine your business goals with your integrity and your values, and that is not an awkward fit. Being fair, being just, realising that people matter more than profit, is not at odds with business – in fact, it helps you to build stronger long-term relationships.

It's also important to be grateful for the support you receive along the way. Don't forget people who gave you a helping hand in the early days, or the way friends and family support you. It all matters. We come into this world with nothing, and we leave with nothing – what matters is enriching the world as you journey through it.

COLIN McKEOWN, MBE

People / Skills / Goals / Succeed / Risk

Drama has always been at the heart of Colin McKeown's life. When he was growing up in a family of nine children, where space, time and even a place to sit were all at a premium, becoming a top TV executive with BAFTA and international Emmy nominations, on top of multiple other awards, seemed like distant impossibilities. Looked upon by partisan Mancunians as a 'Scouse monster who bayed at the moon' in his first job as a broadcast engineer in his 20s, Colin learned early on the tricks of trade which helped him become one of the most respected film and TV producers in the industry. He travelled the world, took risks, pioneered technology, and became a driving force behind some of the most acclaimed television and film to emerge in recent years - eventually earning an MBE for his services to drama production. Now heading an independent production company, LA Productions, Colin shares his views on the importance of good communications, 'going for it' in life, working crazy hours and not waiting for someone to get back to you.

Saying my upbringing was a big influence on me is an understatement. My parents were both very strong characters, and as one of nine it was a family where there wasn't quite enough of everything to go around, so you learned certain skills early on.

You learned how to read people – how to pay attention to body language, how to communicate in a way people would respond to, how to be self-confident enough to go after what you want and not take no for an answer. In fact, it's all down to my mum that I went into TV – at the time, when I was a teenager disillusioned with school, I wanted to go and work at Butlins! But she insisted I go and train at Riversdale, and that early choice – even if it was hers – changed the path my life might have followed.

After college, I joined Granada Studios as a trainee. This was the early 70s and it was based in Manchester, and was the first time I was exposed to people who made me feel not exactly out of my depth, but who I definitely wasn't on the same planet as. They ate different food, they all had degrees, and they talked about mortgages all the time.

> Don't just nibble away at life or your ambitions – go for it.

To try and fit in I reacted by lying. You can shine it up – call it enhancing the details or massaging the truth – but essentially, I lied. When they asked me what my degree was in, I said cyrogenics. So I helped create my own myth. Before that, I was definitely on the receiving end of discrimination – they thought I was some foreign creature, some no-neck Scouse monster who bayed at the moon. There was a huge social gulf, but my fictional cyrogenics degree changed me from 'the Scouser' to 'the Scouse genius'.

It got them off my back and allowed me to learn and evolve at my own pace. That was early on, but it's a vital lesson – in business, in life, you will often find yourself in situations where you feel at a disadvantage. You'll be dealing with people you don't understand,

and may feel held back by that, but you always need to fight it and find a way through it.

I was determined to make it work – and having that laser-like determination is definitely a characteristic that I have, and that I've noticed a lot of successful people have. My dad used to say 'if you want to make it to Birkenhead, aim for the moon', which I always just took as I should aim high. I've set goals, surpassed them, and set new goals – no matter what stage you are at in your career you should be doing that, and be determined to get through the challenges.

Don't just nibble away at life or your ambitions – go for it. I always knew I would amount to something, I always had that self-belief. Some of that is from childhood – being in a big family can make or break you! – and some of it has been learned.

The other thing I think you definitely need to succeed in business is the ability to communicate. When I started at Granada Studios I felt socially inept, but I dealt with it. Then I left the UK and worked in the Middle East and learned even more skills – later in my career I even made a soap opera in Kazakhstan! Living in different cultures, seeing different ways of life, helps with your communication skills. If you can't express yourself, how can you expect other people to understand and respect you?

Working abroad also defined my concept of business. I was involved in filming the Hajj, the great pilgrimage to Mecca. Throughout this great journey, the pilgrims barter – that's how they survive, make money, eat. They trade, they deal, they find out what other people want and make it work for them. They find an angle. I've been doing that ever since.

Nobody succeeds in business without the ability to take risks – the ability to recognise the ones that are worth going for, and to really go for them. It doesn't always work, there will be times when you fail and you might fail very publically, and everyone will see you fail. But it's how you deal with it that counts. You need to remain unafraid; embrace opportunities, technologies, new innovations, new ways of working.

In those early days of Brookside, back in 1982, there were moments where we wondered what the hell we were doing. We did everything differently: we abandoned the old models of TV-making and started our own process. It was unorthodox to say the least. We employed local people with little or no experience, we took chances and ended up with a crew of enthusiastic people who basically had no idea what they were doing!

I was working crazy hours, doing something totally unheard of before in television, and often ended up sleeping in the Brookside houses – I spent the night in pretty much every house on the Close! We also became the first UK TV company to use a Steadicam, which is now standard – me and Phil Redmond went to N.A.B, which is a festival in the States, and brought them back from Los Angeles.

All of it was a risk but we embraced it. We embraced the innovation of the technology, we decided to throw ourselves into this crazy way of working, we did it. And we set goals – initially, one million viewers. When we hit that, we made a cake. Eventually we made it to nine million viewers – we made a TV culture for Liverpool, and trained up people who went on to great things. It left a legacy. Some of those people are still with me, some moved on to become big names in the industry. It might have seemed random and insane at the time but there was method behind our madness. We were working with exciting new talent, with writers like Frank Cottrell Boyce and Jimmy McGovern and Kay Mellor.

For me, those early days sum a lot of it up: we worked hard, we rewrote the rule book, we embraced risk, we used new technology. We were determined. All of those characteristics are essential to success in business – and I still use them today. We were using HD in Kirkdale before anybody else.

Of course risk doesn't always pay off. Sometimes you have moments where you feel like it's going to turn into a disaster. We worked with Lenny Henry on a film called Colour Blind, in honour of Anthony Walker. We decided to use HD for the first time and it was a risk that didn't pay off. We discovered that we'd lost an entire week's

In business, you
have to make
things happen, not
wait for someone
to make it happen
for you.

worth of filming. The whole thing could have ended. But it's low moments like that which define who you are. I didn't give up – I got on the phone to everyone who had been involved, who had given their time for free, and persuaded them to do it all over again.

You have to believe in yourself and your goals and although life can knock some of that out of you, people who succeed always manage to keep hold of that self-belief.

Time and time again I see common characteristics in people who succeed in business: self-confidence, good communication skills, and frankly not suffering fools gladly. They might be softly spoken but there's some quality that makes you think you shouldn't fuck with them!

On the flip side, I see things that hold people back: a lack of self-belief and too much cynicism. Cynicism might be amusing, and a healthy dose of it does no harm, but if you're too cynical, how can you expect your goals and ambitions to break through?

Success, for most people, doesn't come easily. It's rarely something that happens overnight. Even people who have come from privileged backgrounds and go on to succeed in their own right usually take the hard road – if they have a family business, they learn it inside out before they make their mark on it. That's about combining your natural-born skills with hard graft.

I've been asked before if I've changed over the years; if I'd go back and change anything. And essentially, although we all have moments we might look back on and cringe at, the answer is no. Everything you go through, every defeat you face, every time someone discriminates against you or writes you off, every time you fail and come through it – it all adds up to make you who you are.

In some ways, my attitudes have softened over the years, but in some ways they've gotten even tougher. I learned some kind of gypsy skill from my mother for reading people – for weighing them up in thirty seconds. Sometimes I'm wrong, but not usually. In the early days, say when we were assembling that initial bonkers Brookside crew, it helped me decide who to hire. These days, it helps me in different ways.

I'd say that as you get older, and as you develop more experience in business and in life, the skill set you use changes. When I was young I was full of ambition, and it was based on my own natural self-belief, so that was the tool I used. Now I can add track record into the mix – so that's the tool I use. Essentially, the animal doesn't change, it just operates slightly differently to get what it wants.

I suppose in some ways though I've become less tolerant. I get sick of people saying they're just waiting for someone to get back to them. In business, you have to make things happen, not wait for someone to make it happen for you. Don't waste anything – don't waste time, or words, or effort, or energy. Make it all count.

I always come back, again, to something I was told when I was growing up, in this case by my mother. "The world," she used to say, "moves over people who know the way."

RICHARD ELSE

People / Passion/ Brand / Value / Understanding

A self-confessed 'petrol head', Richard Else was obsessed with cars from a very young age. He bought his first motor – a Triumph Herald – before he could even drive, and joined Jaguar straight from university as a graduate trainee. After more than 20 years with the company, he became operations director of Jaguar Land Rover's award-winning Halewood plant, leading his team through the launch of the new Range Rover Evoque, trebling the workforce to 4,500, and meeting strong global demand for both the Evoque and the Discovery Sport. Now, Richard is international manufacturing operations director, overseeing all Jaguar Land Rover overseas operations. Here he tells us about his management style, learning from your mistakes, and why passion is one of the keys to career success.

My parents always made it clear that they wanted me to go to university. When I was about 12 they sat me down and told me that, from this point on, I'd be doing exams every year until I finished my degree. I think, being honest, they had something else in mind for me, something like a lawyer or an accountant, something they saw as being very respectable and lucrative - and not too stressful!

In the end, though, there was really only one choice for me. I'd always been obsessed with cars. Before I was even 10, I used to watch Ian Ogilvy in The Saint on TV, and loved his Jag – maybe I'll have one of those one day, I thought. I saved up and bought my first car a year before I was even old enough to drive – it was always a passion.

So when I finished my degree, and I was looking at the jobs out there that I could go for, the motor industry was really the only one I was interested in. I was lucky enough to get a place on a graduate trainee scheme at Jaguar, and I'm still here 27 years on.

I think that's so important, following your passion. We all want to be paid well – we all have bills and families and responsibilities. Being ambitious for nothing but money or prestige though doesn't give you the same satisfaction, in my opinion.

For me, that sense of satisfaction is vital. I am still so very, very proud to say I work for Jaguar Land Rover. To work for a business that makes headlines in all the right ways. To be involved in a globally renowned brand and product. I don't think I would have stayed for as long as I have unless I had that passion.

It's also a very competitive industry – it's tough. You often work long hours, and there are always fresh challenges. I can honestly say it's always interesting – no two days pan out quite as you expect them to and, for me, that's also part of the appeal. It's why I keep on pushing to do my very best. I once went for an interview with another company – a pet food manufacturer – a couple of years after I joined Jaguar, but all it did was make me realise how much I wanted to stay!

I've worked in all of the company's UK locations, and I started in advanced manufacture engineering in Coventry. I know the business inside out, I understand the nitty gritty, and I've come all the way up through the same organisation. That helps me to have a better understanding of my team, it gives me credibility, and means I have a big network – all of this has contributed to my career path.

One of the things I learned early on was that I'm not the kind of boss who bangs his fist on the desk. I like to engage with people. I like people! My management style tends to be consultative rather than confrontational – I think it makes better sense to get on with people, and get the best out of them. As far as I'm concerned, there are more than 4,000 people working at Halewood, which means 4,000 people who can help things run better, who have ideas, who have potential. Whatever level someone is at in the organisation, I'm interested, I like to have a friendly chat, let them know they're valued. I think it gives people a sense of ownership and involvement that is beneficial to the whole business.

> It's not just about telling them what to do, it's about allowing them to decide what to do themselves.

I also think it's essential to take inspiration from the people around you – the things they do right and, very occasionally, the things they do wrong maybe! I've been very lucky in my career to have bosses who have coached and mentored me, and taught me such a lot along the way, but you have to be willing to listen and learn. You have to stay alert, listen when you are wrong, make the most of their experience. I had one boss who told me my only job was to make him look good – and the payback was that his responsibility to me was to train me up to take his boss's job!

Now, I am able to pass some of that on, to coach and mentor others. It's not just about telling them what to do, it's about allowing them to decide what to do themselves. Sharing an anecdote – even if it shows a weakness, or is about a time something went wrong – lets them know you are human, and allows them to reflect better on their own position. I always value new people who come into the business with a fresh pair of eyes, with a different perspective.

Other lessons you learn as you go, often when things go wrong - or not as well as you had perhaps wanted them to. Or, of course, when you are simply in a really difficult position and have to do things you don't want to do.

> We all find ourselves in tight spots, and we all make mistakes. The only thing you can do is acknowledge them, learn from them, and try not to make the same ones again!

There are tough situations faced by people in business all the time - it is part of the job. But some are definitely tougher than others. For me, I think the all time low came in 2008, when the global recession hit us, and lots of other companies, very hard. Lots of businesses had to make some difficult decisions that year.

I remember sitting in front of people who had worked there for years, breaking the news that they were at risk of redundancy. It was horrible, frankly. You can prepare yourself in some ways – know the facts, understand their situation, try and be supportive – but nobody can really prepare you for the human toll, or the way individuals might react in a situation like that.

We all find ourselves in tight spots, and we all make mistakes. The only thing you can do is acknowledge them, learn from them, and try not to make the same ones again! The way the Halewood plant has developed is an immense source of pride to me, being able to take it into the next phase of its success - but it hasn't all been perfect.

When we were overseeing the launch of the Evoque, I wish we'd spent more time preparing people, explaining what we were trying to achieve. It was the biggest car in the factory's history, and it was their first time making a Range Rover. Not everybody understood.

After that, we did more – new recruits are given brand training, so they have a better understanding of the product and its customers. Brand needs to mean something to staff as well as customers, and that's something we've worked on.

I suppose as both my career and my life outside work have moved on, I've had to find different ways to balance things. When you're very young and just starting out, everything is about work – you can work all the hours, it's all that matters. But as you get older, and if you have a family, you learn the value of switching off as well. You can't be successful in business without facing stressful situations, but you also need to be able to turn it off and think about something else, for your own mental health. These days, I tend to start work between 5 and 5.30am, so I can finish at 6pm and go home. I try and preserve time at the weekends. It's actually one of the ways you continue to love your job – by keeping it fresh.

I love my work, and being in charge at Halewood. I think I have plenty left to give to Jaguar Land Rover, ways to support its massive growth ambitions.

I've loved working for this company. There were times, when I was younger, when I considered striking out on my own, starting my own business, but the timing was never right, and perhaps I wasn't quite brave enough.

But now, with hindsight, I know I made the right decision. I followed my passion, and I found the right fit – and now I find my work immensely rewarding. I'm sure my 15-year-old self would have been pretty pleased with the outcome!

PETER JACKSON

People / Leader / Team / Successful / Instincts

Joining a law firm straight from graduation, Peter Jackson was in his 30s when his personal ambitions 'kicked in'. After that, he worked his way up to become the Managing Partner of Hill Dickinson – one of the top 30 law firms in the UK, with bases in three continents, a turnover of more than £100m and 1250 employees. Here he shares his views on the challenges of leadership, adapting to the changing landscape of business, the emotional toll that being in charge can bring and the ways that your competitors can actually be your biggest allies.

Law is a very self-obsessed profession, especially when you first start out. You focus so much on building up your name, your reputation, your career. You do well for your firm because that reflects well on you – and it's all about you.

I was the same when I started out. I came straight from law school to Hill Dickinson and, although I had a team of people I worked with, it was all about me. I make no apologies for that – it's the way it needs to be in the beginning.

It was only when I was in my 30s that I started to recognise that I could do more, that I needed more. I needed to be stimulated and challenged in a way that just being a successful individual lawyer at a successful firm couldn't provide. I realised that moving up within the organisation was what I wanted – and that it was something I would care about, and be passionate about, and be good at.

Since then, there has been a lot to be proud of. Growing turnover, opening new offices here and overseas, leading significant mergers and acquisitions, and overseeing Hill Dickinson's strategic development.

But there have also been moments that have been difficult – devastating even. I've made mistakes. The firm has made mistakes. Tough, frightening times happen to everyone involved in business; to everyone in life. It's how you cope with those times that counts – not only making the right decisions and doing the right thing, but being able to sleep at night and hold your head high.

> At the end of the day, every leader is different, and every situation is different.

For us, one of the biggest challenges came as a result of the recession of 2008. That changed everything in the legal sector – everything. Up until that point, it was hard to be a lawyer and not be successful. People had solicitors for life, they played golf with them, it was a done deal. But the recession meant that the commercial sector – property, banking, insurance, corporate – started to re-examine things.

People stopped litigating as much to avoid paying lawyers; we all had to start looking at pricing, at services, at re-negotiating contracts. The gravy train came to a very sudden halt and a lot of very big firms went under. Other firms started looking for work they would have previously considered beneath them – which affected everyone else. It became a buyers' market and clients were scrutinising exactly what they needed, and how much they had to pay for it.

We reacted slowly – too slowly, with hindsight. It wasn't until a few years later that it became obvious we couldn't go on. Hill Dickinson was, for want of a better word, a 'nice' firm. We were like an overgrown family. We'd hoped to ride out the storm, but by 2012 it was obvious we couldn't – and in 2013, we had to lose around 150 people over a six to eight month period.

That is something no leader wants to face – but it's your job. As a leader, I actually regret that we left it so long before we took action. The situation got worse the more time we let go by. I remember sitting in a meeting with someone I'd worked with almost 30 years, explaining the situation and why we had to let him go. I didn't know which of us was going to burst into tears first.

But I learned from it. I learned how important it is to adapt to a changing business landscape – to a changing economic climate. I learned how important it is to do your research, see what is going on, and to act effectively and quickly. I learned that you need to be able to divorce the personal and the commercial – and that I wasn't very good at it to start off with!

I also learned how important it is to treat people with respect and with dignity. It might not make the reality of the situation any better, but it helps. If you are sure you are making the right commercial decision, then treat that person with empathy – because that is how you will sleep at night.

Sometimes there is simply no replacement for experience when it comes to leadership. There are hundreds of theories about it, and examples of ways other leaders have dealt with situations but, at the end of the day, every leader is different, and every situation is different. Getting things right is never guaranteed – but there are things you can do to help yourself.

I'm a firm believer that 'he who does the most homework wins' – know your stuff! At the end of the day, you will be called on to make difficult judgement calls. By their very nature, they depend on your judgement, which is a blend of experience, natural instincts and gut feel. But you will definitely improve your odds of making the right call if you have the right information in front of you – it's about trusting your instincts but not being ruled by them.

> **He who does the most homework wins.**

There isn't always a right and a wrong answer – sometimes you'll get it right, and other times, for a variety of reasons both inside and outside of your control, you'll get it wrong.

It's vital that you allow yourself to make those mistakes – and that you admit to them. When I first moved into senior management, I made mistakes, everyone does. But you need to 'fess up, explain what went wrong and why, and look at how you can fix it. Lying to people and trying to cover up that mistake, or blaming someone else, is the absolute worst thing you can do – people will never trust you again.

It's also vital, as a leader, to realise that you are not alone. Yes, the buck might stop with you – but you are surrounded by a team. If you've got any sense, you'll make that a great team – you'll surround yourself with people who are cleverer than you! I'm not an expert in HR, or IT, or any number of things, but I make sure I have access to people who are. As a leader, you're the one who has to make the big decisions, and stand up and take the flak – but you are not alone. Don't fall into the trap of thinking that you have to do everything yourself – nobody is that good!

You need to be self-aware – whatever is lacking in your make-up, look for it in others. If you think you need help – training, mentoring, coaching – then don't be afraid to admit it and act on it. If you expect yourself to be perfect at everything, you'll fail. Like with football, just because you're the captain of the team, you don't have to be the one who takes all the penalties. Get a good – no, a great – number two, and build a fantastic team of skilled people you can trust.

> **If you expect yourself to be perfect at everything, you'll fail.**

Building that team is one of the most important things you will do as a leader. I think I have good judgement about people, good instincts. You need to develop those instincts, and see beyond who you like and think you would work well with, to who would contribute to the team. I like grafters, people who are willing to really put in the effort. That's something that's lost a little in this generation – not everyone who works in IT can be a Mark Zuckerberg. Not everyone who launches a company will be Steve Jobs – these are the whizz kids, the geniuses who would probably have been successful whatever they did. Most of us need to work harder and longer!

Most leaders do have good instincts about people – but you have to work on that. If you don't learn how to get the most out of people, to motivate and inspire them, you won't get the best out of them. And don't treat everyone the same – your people are all individuals, and you need to know that if you're going to create an environment where they, and your business, can succeed.

You need to be able to manipulate people, in the nicest possible way. I wasn't a natural at this when I started, but I've learned along the way.

I've also learned that your competitors, people who in business are your opponents, don't need to be your enemies. Early on I joined an organisation where people can network and share experiences. You might be at war with people in business, but you can learn from them. If people are willing to share, you can pick up great hints and tips. If you're facing an especially difficult situation and don't know what to do, they might have faced it before. I had a tough challenge with two very valuable colleagues who were not getting on – it seemed as though we would end up losing one, which we really didn't want to do. By speaking to a managing partner at one of our biggest rivals, I got some valuable advice that gave me a fresh perspective, and helped to calm the whole situation down.

Your competitors, if they are willing to share and if you are in return, can actually be your allies in leadership – so don't be blinkered about building those relationships.

As you go through your career and experience different situations, and meet different people, you also get a clearer idea of the reasons certain people fail – which can help you avoid the same pitfalls! You can't be selfish, for one – if you want to be a leader, you have to see the bigger picture. If you're managing your own team, or you're part of a bigger organisation, you can't focus only on what your team needs. You need to look at the benefits of cross-selling, or building relationships that benefit the whole company. You get much more out of life if you collaborate – and if you can't see beyond your own needs, you'll never move on.

The same is true about an obsession with money. We all want to be well paid for what we do – but there are other ways to add value. Corporate social responsibility shouldn't just be a box you tick – it should have real meaning. Greed can bring good people down – if you are obsessed only with money, you will lose your people skills, your empathy, your ability to work for a business made up of hundreds of people and not just you. There is no such thing as a personally greedy leader, it's simply incompatible and unsustainable – leaders are ambitious for everyone they are responsible for, not just themselves.

That's one of the things that does become clearer as you get older and more experienced. You become more aware of leaving a legacy, and of how important it is that your business succeeds. A lot of hugely successful law firms went down after the recession. People lost their livelihoods. I was in a meeting with one firm as we were taking on some of their staff and work, and they were relieved to even be getting paid that month – it brings it home to you that you have a huge responsibility. That's not easy, and if you're not up for it, then don't even think about becoming a leader because it's part of the job – and yes, personally, I do think it's worth it.

As a leader, you have to accept that responsibility. You have to train yourself not to panic when things go wrong, and to know when to forge ahead and take risk. You need to surround yourself with that fantastic team, and all those people who are cleverer than you. And you need to acknowledge how clever you are – bad things happen every day. A good leader will deal with those bad things, and still have a smile on their face in the lift, or a good morning for the receptionist.

A good leader will have confidence in themselves, and faith in their abilities – remember that you are a leader because you're clever too. Because you're charismatic. You know your sector. You believe in yourself. No matter how you feel inside, get a grip, get any help you need, and trust yourself in the same way all those people you have responsibility for are trusting you – because you are a leader, and that's your job.

SARA WILDE MCKEOWN

People / Learn / Belief / Inquisitive / Willing

Sara Wilde McKeown started her business career with Trinity Mirror in the 1980s, with 'more confidence than competence', before eventually rising up to become the youngest, and only, female MD of one of the country's largest regional publishers. She is now Managing Director of Influential, a leading communications firm with bases across the UK and clients which include Camelot, NHS England and Stagecoach. Here she tells us about early mistakes, learning from the best, and the challenges of providing leadership in difficult times.

When I started my career, I think I ran entirely on arrogance, if I'm honest. I don't mean that I was an awful person – I just had a lot of self-belief and determination. I was probably operating with more confidence than competence, but I was also always willing to learn, always open to ideas. I found myself as part of this big company and had every faith that, when the opportunities came my way, I'd be able to take them and make my mark.

> We've all seen very clever people achieve very little because they don't quite believe they can do it – and we've all seen people who are as thick as two short planks march successfully through life on spirit and hard work alone.

You need that innate belief to move on in life. We've all seen very clever people achieve very little because they don't quite believe they can do it – and we've all seen people who are as thick as two short planks march successfully through life on spirit and hard work alone. There are no rules, and there is no right answer, as to whether successful people are born or created.

Certainly, though, I've noticed some things that these success stories all seem to have in common. One is self-belief – and the other is being inquisitive. People who do well tend to be interested in other people, in the world around them – they're always looking for ways to do better than the last time, or to improve.

I count myself as a positive person, but I have been told that sometimes I never seem to be satisfied. I'll look at something and say 'well, that's great, I love that – but what if we'd done it this way'? And 'how about if we try this next time'? That springs from being inquisitive, from striving to do something better – and let's face it, the human race wouldn't have moved on much if it wasn't for that type of thinking. I believe that a healthy dose of well-managed dissatisfaction can be a very useful quality – especially if it is tempered by self-awareness.

It also gives you a certain resilience, I think, which you need in business. Early on in my career I was asked if I knew much about computers, and if I'd like to go and run a new magazine operation in the Midlands. They needed my answer that day and I had to move the week after – but I said yes.

After, when I'd accepted, I started to think 'hang on, I've never been an MD before...and I don't actually know that much computers...', but I did it. That's the self-belief – being willing to take a chance on your own abilities, to take a step into the unknown.

The resilience is what I needed later – when I arrived to find a grotty office above a deli in Solihull, and 15 staff. I honestly could have cried when I got there. But I threw myself into it, let myself be inquisitive and dissatisfied, and pushed ahead – within 18 months we had had 120 staff, 11 titles and brand new purpose-built offices.

That time in my life also led on to me getting some fantastic advice. Sometimes, when you are young especially, you forge ahead and get carried away with yourself. The performance figures weren't great, and I was worried. I went to see the Financial Director of the whole group, and said 'look, I think I've cocked up here – we've done too much, too soon'.

He told me that coming off the corners occasionally was all part of business – and if you don't come off the corners, you're not going fast enough! His job, in the more senior role, was to put up the safety barriers and stop me crashing out of the race. I've always remembered that, and think I was very lucky to be in an environment where I could learn from some very clever, experienced and supportive people.

That's a vital part of business, I think – always learning. Soak everything up, learn, always be on the lookout for something useful you can tuck away and use later. I've had a long and very varied career and worked with some greats – and I've always listened. Even when you're young, and someone might seem a bit long in the tooth and irrelevant, there is something they can share with you. Now, running my own business, part of me is the Grand Dame with all the experience to share – a whole back catalogue of highs, lows and stories to draw on. But sometimes I'm also still the person who goes 'sod it, let's have some fun'!

The 'sod it' attitude doesn't always work, but making mistakes is part of what will make you a better business person. You have to be willing to graft, to be determined, but also to accept that things will go wrong – and learn how to cope when they do. Go into risky situations with eyes wide open, aware that they might not work out, but confident enough to know that you'll survive and that you will learn.

I think, as I've become older and more experienced, some views have changed. When I came back to the regions, at MD level, I realised how much of a responsibility that role brought with it. I've always been interested in business and politics and economic development and, when you are in the media, you have a vital part to play. I had to start asking myself whether what we were doing was contributing – not just an employer, but as an influencer. Were we helping the area to flourish?

I've also learned that being a leader – whether that's in the corporate world, or in your own business – isn't something you can ever switch off from. You can't decide you're not going to bother to lead one day, because you're struggling, or in a challenging situation – that's when people need you the most.

As an example, I was in a position where we took a very hard decision to close down the printing presses in Liverpool and move that function elsewhere. This was a decision taken at a higher level, that I respected, but didn't necessarily agree with – the symbolism of it, the loss of jobs, all weighed very heavily on me. I also didn't like the way they were trying to handle it, and had to ask for space to deal with that my own way.

Leading through a difficult time is hard enough – but leading when it's a difficult choice you don't truly agree with is awful. But what can you do? You can't just shrug and say 'it's not my fault – I told them

I didn't agree'. You have a responsibility to lead people through the maze – it's your job to rally the troops, to find a shared vision, to give them a future to believe in, even if their present doesn't feel too good. You have to quickly re-calibrate, adapt, find that vision that will help everyone.

Eventually I decided to leave Trinity Mirror. I'd worked in the same industry for over 20 years, and taking the next step was both exciting and frightening.

But I genuinely believe that we are all capable of changing paths. You can take your skills and experience and apply them to a different sector, or a different role – you don't have to be stuck. Sometimes, again, it is about having the self-belief to make that kind of move.

I'd always thought that one day I'd be involved in my own business and was looking for something with potential, something with a solid core that I could help to grow, and I found that with Influential. We have a great team, we're expanding and have some brilliant clients – and I still feel inquisitive. As well as our strategy for the company, I'm very hands-on, getting involved in client projects and spouting off about everything I've learned from them – I see it as another opportunity to learn, to soak things up, to add to my experience. It's good to still feel capable of getting enthused and carried away, to still be so interested in what is going on around me.

It also feels good, after all those years in the corporate world, to have my own place and be making my own decisions. It takes guts to start a business – and I have huge respect for anybody young doing it, starting out on their own, having that belief. I did it after years of experience, and it still takes guts! The advantage of doing it my way, though, is that I've been able to learn from the very best – and apply that learning to what I'm doing now.

The communications sector is fast-moving. Digital, print, video – it's ever-evolving. And that's how I like to think my career will be too – I'm onto my second path now, and I wouldn't be surprised if I end up with a third before I'm done!

MATT BUCKLEY

People / Understand / Change / Team / Goals

Matt Buckley joined historic UK glass manufacturer Pilkington as a graduate trainee, freely admitting that, at that stage in his life, he still had no idea what he wanted to be when he grew up! These days, after working his way through the company, he is very much the grown up – managing director of the entire UK architectural business, responsible for 1200 employees and an integral part of the future of Pilkington. Here Matt reflects on how to bring about corporate change, leading a business through tough times and the qualities that he feels have helped him move onwards and upwards.

> **One person cannot drag a whole business uphill. You simply can't do it alone.**

I left university with an English degree and no real idea what to do next. I liked the idea of being a professional footballer, but sadly a lack of sufficient skill let me down on that front!

I was interested in sales and marketing, and I had a leaning towards companies that were manufacturers – businesses that made stuff seemed more appealing, somehow. I applied to a few different companies, the big names of the day, but in the end went with Pilkington because they offered a really good training programme that I thought would set me up with some great skills and experience for the rest of my career. At that stage I assumed I would be moving on, as most people do.

That was in 1987 and I'm still here, albeit in a very different role. Every time I found myself thinking I should perhaps move on and look at fresh opportunities elsewhere, something new came up, a better opportunity, or the chance to develop a new role. Part of that was just timing, part of that was simply that we are a good fit, perhaps.

If I'm asked why it is that I've been promoted at different times, or given these new opportunities, I'd like to think a lot of it is down to attitude. I've consistently demonstrated a positive attitude, good communication, and individual values that work well with corporate values.

For me, one of the key requirements in business is the ability to involve everyone, whether that's a small team you lead near the start of your career, or the whole company. One person cannot drag a whole business uphill. You simply can't do it alone.

That, combined with hard work and ambition, have helped me to rise through the company ranks. There is nothing wrong with being ambitious and results-driven – there are ways you can do that without standing on other people along the way. You can move up in the right way, with integrity, and decent behaviour.

Now, I realise that having been so immersed in the company for so long, and also having worked in lots of different teams and places, can be an advantage. I am steeped in the history and culture of Pilkington – which gives me the edge over someone who has just parachuted in.

But it also means that I constantly need to work at keeping a fresh pair of eyes – keeping things fresh, being able to see things from different perspectives.

The trick is, I suppose, combining that with my experience and the trust and respect of my team. That respect and trust is essential, especially when a business is going through challenging times, like we have been.

We have a fabulous reputation and a great heritage, but the reality is that, in our business, we now face competitors with much lower costs. We can't rely on brand alone. We've had to rationalise. We've had to change, at a corporate level. We've had to become much more customer-focused, looking at ways to offer added value.

There are always issues – for example, we had an entire float line dedicated to producing glass for solar panels and for various reasons, almost overnight, the need for that disappeared.

We need to be agile and responsive, to be able to react quickly to economic factors. To do that, we needed change at a fundamental level.

None of this has been easy. We have had to reorganise to survive, and we are still nowhere near where we need to be financially – simply not going under has been an achievement. We've survived and now we need to thrive. We are owned by a Japanese company and we need to continue to strive to add significant value, to deliver the best we can.

We are a strong UK brand within a global company – but at the moment, in all honesty, our past is stronger than our present. The challenge for us is to ensure our future lives up to our heritage.

Leading a business in a situation like this requires a calm head. It requires good communication. You are responsible for the health and safety of your employees, for their livelihoods, for the continued future of this historic brand.

You either feel paralysed by the enormity of all of that, or you believe in your abilities, the abilities of your team and the future of your business.

For me, communication is at the heart of it. This business has worked for decades in siloes, different geographical locations - we now have 14 different sites, different teams, different personnel, all with different goals and cultures.

If we're going to live up to our past, and to our corporate vision and values, that had to change. Change, of course, doesn't happen overnight and sometimes I struggle with that, I can be impatient and I have to bite my tongue. I have to accept that we are breaking the habits of people's whole lifetimes.

I can be talking to a guy who has done things a certain way for 40 years – why should I expect him to suddenly change his mind and do it my way? And why do I assume that, just because something makes perfect sense to me, it makes sense to him?

Leading change isn't about forcing something – it's about involving everybody, explaining why change is necessary, what the future will look like and getting them to buy into it. Again, you can't do it alone. This is a team sport! This is one of the key differences between being a manager and being a leader – the former is largely about processes, the latter is about passion.

You need to be able to communicate your goals and that passion in a language that all of your audiences understand. I have visited the different sites personally, met people face to face – even if that means I've had to go and talk to the night shift in Glasgow at 10pm.

If you want your people to invest in those goals, you have to show them that they are also their goals. Be honest, but be reassuring. Give people the chance to vent or ask questions. Avoid jargon, and don't speak in acronyms that not everybody will understand. Communicate clearly – and talk, rather than relying on email!

> Opening yourself up to others is not a sign of weakness – recognising when you need some support is a sign of strength.

Not everyone will agree with your message – in our case, how to be Best in Glass - but by at least communicating it clearly, and ensuring that everybody understands it, you will vastly improve your odds.

I think a lot of leadership is about translating your own passion, and corporate aims, into a language that people understand. Show them that even though they are all in different teams, doing different things, they are all united by one thing – the customer at the end of the process. Harness your own enthusiasm, share it, show people where they fit in to the big picture, and how important they are.

If somebody doesn't understand, why don't they understand? Is it my fault for not communicating it properly? How can I do it differently? There is a big difference between somebody not fully understanding what you are asking of them and somebody wilfully ignoring it – don't judge until you know which one it is.

The power of the person at the top being positive and honest has a huge effect on the whole company. It helps to energise people, to enthuse them, but also to show them the reality of situations and the need to not be complacent. I'm in charge – they don't need to hear me moaning about how hard it all is. They need to hear me addressing the challenges and telling them how we can work better, and asking them to play their part in it that process.

It's all about learning to keep your ears open – always be willing to listen and to learn. Be aware of the impact of your attitude on people and the way your body language communicates as well as your words.

I also think it's essential to be willing to admit your mistakes. Organisations display learned behaviours. I believe in being as honest as possible, and take the attitude that 'mistake' is another word for 'learning'.

Admit your mistakes. Explain why they happened. Discuss what you've learned from them. If you do that, you are informally coaching your entire team to do the same – getting away from a culture of fear, where people are scared to admit they've done something wrong. If you want people to be brave and transparent and accept responsibility for their actions, then you have to display that behaviour yourself – the big stick never gets you as far as collaboration.

A lot of business is also about building solid relationships and allegiances, and finding people you trust. I don't want to work with time wasters or backstabbers. I want to work with people who are aligned to what we are trying to achieve, and who will work with me to reach those goals.

Sometimes, you need to reach out, to get support, and that's where those relationships become even more vital. Recently, I faced a very difficult situation involving some key people who announced they were leaving at the same time. Not only were they leaving, but they were leaving to go and work for a competitor, so they had to go on gardening leave straight away and that left a huge gap in our structure.

It really threw me off my game. I had sleepless nights. I was anxious. At first I wasn't sure what to do, so I asked for help. I spoke to trusted colleagues and friends, and shared some of my concerns.

The response was amazing. They were so helpful. People contacted me to see what they could do to help, or they simply listened and offered advice. Opening yourself up to others is not a sign of weakness – recognising when you need some support is a sign of strength.

I've been with Pilkington for the whole of my working life and can honestly say that I am still passionate about my job. I'm passionate about the people I work with, about the brand, and about improving the way we deliver. If you cut me open, I'd probably have Pilkington running through the centre, like a stick of rock.

I have never had one of those Sunday nights where I dread going into the office the next day. I've never had that sick feeling as the working week begins. Perhaps if I start to, I'll know that it's finally time to move elsewhere!

GARY MILLAR

People / Positive / Luck / Hard Work / Mistakes

Gary Millar's childhood and teenage years were far from easy. In and out of foster homes, and later caring for sick parents, he had more than his fair share of difficulties. However, instead of defeating his passion for life, all those challenges sparked an entrepreneurial spirit which helped define who he is today. Now Gary is regarded as one of top 50 LGBT executives in the UK, and is a renowned motivational speaker. He was the first serving Lord Mayor to be 'out', and is also a co-owner of Parr Street, the Grammy award-winning studio and hotel complex once owned by Genesis, and favoured by the likes of Echo and the Bunnymen, Black Sabbath, Coldplay and Rihanna. Here he shares his views on why it's necessary to make mistakes and why fighting adversity is the key to the positive learning experiences that allow success.

I've worked in business myself for many years, and have also met a lot of successful business people in my time. I've often found that they have something that drives them, that motivates them – that pushes them just that little bit further than others are pushed.

For me, a lot of that motivation came from my childhood. By the time I was 11, I had been in eight different foster homes. I was always the new boy at school, and I was called a dunce and mocked. That sort of thing can have all kinds of effects on a person, but for me, it made me strive – I wanted to escape that feeling, that vulnerability, and have always strived not to go back to it.

I was always dressed in hand-me-downs, which was another reason I was picked on – and even to this day, I like to dress well, present myself well. It's all part of taking pride in what I do.

By the age of 12, I had four different jobs – paper rounds and running errands and the like – so I suppose you could say I had a strong work ethic and an entrepreneurial outlook from an early age. Back then, the motivation was simple: working hard earned me money, and having money allowed me to buy my own clothes, make my own choices, and have some self-respect. It was part of an early plan to rescue myself from embarrassment, and I quite soon made the connection between hard work and improving my situation.

> **People are always very keen to listen to the negatives, and ignore the positives, whether it's about themselves or about others.**

Those challenges were during my formative years, but that drive, that ambition, has never left me. These days, though, it's not just drive and ambition for myself on a personal level – it's for the people I work with, the place I live, for my community.

I am still very active in my own business life, but in addition these days, I enjoy supporting others on their journeys. I find it very rewarding and think it's important to be aware of ways you can give back in life. That's what I needed back when I was a kid – not to be told I was thick, or to be humiliated, but to be given some support and told that someone believed in me. I've learned not to judge others, to try and understand their circumstances and to give them the benefit of the doubt, and to be positive. People are always very keen to listen to the negatives, and ignore the positives, whether it's about themselves or about others.

Turning that corner in my own life, finding the self-belief I needed, allowed me to pursue my business ambitions. I strongly believe that a positive attitude, hard work, and the willingness to take opportunities when they present themselves contribute to success a lot more than luck or being in the right place at the right time. But I can understand why people think it's down to luck – because being positive and being lucky tend to go hand in hand. Funnily enough, you often find that they gravitate towards each other, so you find them in the same place! Successful business people often act as catalysts – they bring people together, they make things happen, they're not afraid to be challenged or to embrace change. They're listeners, they have empathy, and they learn from their mistakes.

> **Being positive and being lucky tend to go hand in hand.**

I made a lot of mistakes along the way in my business career, but all of them contributed to who I am now, and the experience I have to share when I'm working with other entrepreneurs. In 1985, I started an IT business writing apps and selling them to golf clubs. It was all going well, but six months later the technology they used became obsolete. That was out of my control, but it taught me a valuable lesson about not putting all of your eggs in one basket, or developing a product that is entirely reliant on an outside supplier. Since then, I've tried to work on the rule of never being more than 30% dependent on one supplier or one customer. That was learned the hard way, and it also taught me about the importance of sustainability over the long term. One minute I was successful, the next it was over.

Another mistake that turned out to be very positive was taking a position with the Apple Centre without really researching what I was going to be doing there and what the role involved. In the end I was only there for eight weeks, as it just didn't suit me at all, but while I was there I sold £400,000 worth of computers. That taught me how to sell – and ultimately, being able to sell is a vital skill in business.

Later on in life, I had a new project – the International Festival of Motorsport with Stirling Moss at Aintree Racecourse's historic Grand Prix track. I put far too much money into it, and lost far too much as well, but thought it would be all right as I'd recoup the losses the year after. Except that Aintree was redeveloping, which threw a huge spanner in the works. That taught me about the importance of doing your homework, doing your due diligence and research and not simply getting carried away with enthusiasm for a good idea. Taking a risk is one thing, but it needs to be informed risk.

I went on trying new things, new ventures, and I went on making those mistakes – because without the mistakes you never learn. As long as it is a different mistake each time, you need to try and be positive about it. You might not see the benefits until some time has passed, but they will be there, clear to see, with hindsight. Your failures will teach you some very valuable lessons. If nothing else, they will teach you how to move on, how to re-engineer, how to cope when things don't go exactly to plan, and how to be resilient. You also learn that success can be measured in many different ways – it's not all about money.

Back in the early 90s, I started IT & training business Computer Centres UK, which still exists today, as well as working on a labour of love – co-rescuing the historic Parr Street Studios in Liverpool, where some of the biggest names in the music business have recorded. That was about more than business, or money – it was about protecting jobs, saving the building, supporting the industry, it was the right time. That wasn't one of my failures, and I'm very proud of it, but it did teach me a lot about teamwork, about disrupting the market, original thinking and challenging the norm. If you get the right plans, the right team in place, people who share your vision and your ethics, and you give them responsible autonomy, a business can run itself.

Business might, to the outside observer, be about money – but for me it is about a lot more than that. I've learned some of my most important life lessons through business enterprises, and the people I've met in business. Society is made up of many different types of people and it's important that commerce reflects that – diversity in the workplace isn't just something that sounds good, it's absolutely essential. You can't understand your customers without understanding society, and businesses should have a bigger purpose than shareholder returns. They should also be about social value, about positive change, about having real purpose.

For me, now, after all of those ups and downs, that remains at the heart of what I want to do in both business and in life. To get out there and do some good. To create some opportunities as well as take them. To make a difference.

THANK YOU